The Creativity Workbook for Coaches and Creatives

In this practical workbook, creativity coaches from around the world share their best exercises to help the reader meet the demands of the creative process, the creative personality, and the creative life.

This book is packed with an extensive list of exercises that have been vetted by coaches working on the frontlines of creativity, and tried, tested, and proven effective with coaching clients. The hands-on activities cover a wide range of common challenges, including creative blocks and resistance, waning and lost motivation, making time for creating, the pain of disappointment, and more. This guide recognizes the connections between mental health and an alive creativity, and includes helpful advice from professionals who actively and regularly work with individual creatives on issues of process, productivity, motivation, and career.

Ideal for coaches and therapists, as well as creatives in every discipline, this book is a valuable aid for achieving creative realization.

Eric Maisel, PhD, is a retired family therapist, active creativity coach, and the author of more than fifty books including *Coaching the Artist Within* and *Secrets of a Creativity Coach*.

The Creativity Workbook for Coaches and Creatives

50+ Inspiring Exercises From Creativity Coaches Worldwide

EDITED BY ERIC MAISEL

Routledge
Taylor & Francis Group

NEW YORK AND LONDON

First published 2020
by Routledge
52 Vanderbilt Avenue, New York, NY 10017

and by Routledge
2 Park Square, Milton Park, Abingdon, Oxon, OX14 4RN

Routledge is an imprint of the Taylor & Francis Group, an informa business

Library of Congress Cataloging-in-Publication Data
A catalog record for this book has been requested

ISBN: 978-0-367-37492-1 (hbk)
ISBN: 978-0-367-37493-8 (pbk)
ISBN: 978-0-429-35470-0 (ebk)

Typeset in Avenir and Sabon
by Apex CoVantage, LLC

Contents

Introduction

Every coach (like, ultimately, every therapist or other helper) invents his or her way of working with clients. Personally, I've worked as a creativity coach for the past thirty years, learning from my clients, discerning which tactics and strategies work and which don't, and inventing the territory as I went.

During that time, I've written more than twenty books for creatives, including *Coaching the Artist Within, Unleashing the Artist Within, Fearless Creating, The Creativity Book, The Van Gogh Blues, Mastering Creative Anxiety*, and *Creative Recovery*.

Each of these books contained exercises for creatives to try out. Personally, I believe in exercises, especially simple ones that are easy to understand and easy to try. I've heard from countless readers how valuable this or that exercise proved. Even an exercise as simple as "Please think about what you just read" can reap real dividends!

Of course, some coaches would never dream of providing clients with exercises. They wouldn't think of trying out an exercise in session or suggesting to a client that he or she might try out a certain exercise at home, either optionally or as homework. But many coaches are very easy with providing clients with exercises, using exercises in the groups they run, including exercises in the books they write, and employing exercises to keep their own creative life on track.

Those coaches who do use exercises have something useful to share with their fellow coaches and with creatives in all the disciplines, as the exercises they employ have been tested in the crucible of coaching. Real creatives have tried them out. Such exercises are not abstract lessons in what might work but exercises that have been tested with clients.

Covering a wide range of common challenges, including creative blocks, resistance, waning motivation, self-defeating self-talk, the pain of criticism and disappointments, and more, these exercises can help all coaches more effectively coach their creative clients and help creatives better meet the demands of the creative process, the creative personality, and the creative life.

"Creativity" is the word we've come to use to stand for some of our most important human talents and traits. It stands for our ability to problem-solve and innovate, the way we manifest our potential, the ingredient we need to flourish at work, and one of the most important ways that we make meaning and experience life as purposeful.

Today, it is something that just about everyone wants and needs more of. Even clients who aren't self-identified creative or performing artists or who don't bring up creativity as an issue can still markedly benefit from exercises designed to help them maintain a regular practice, break through resistance and get to their important tasks, and increase their discipline, devotion, imagination, and productivity.

Indeed, creativity may be the most important life skill of the 21st century. As such, *The Creativity Workbook for Coaches and Creatives* is a useful book that will aid creatives and those, like creativity coaches, life coaches, therapists, and other helpers, whose job it is to help them. And it is very special in the following regard.

Books that provide creativity exercises are typically written by a single individual who creates the exercises out of his or her imagination but who rarely gets to see how those exercises actually work with flesh-and-blood creatives. If the exercises are employed at all, they are usually only employed in a workshop setting. Now that the profession of creativity coaching has been in existence for some years, that situation has changed.

Now there are professional creativity coaches who regularly work with individual creative and performing artists and other creatives on issues of process, productivity, motivation, and career. These coaches try things out and see how well their exercises do or don't work. They get feedback from their clients and see results. This makes *The Creativity Workbook for Coaches and Creatives* a unique contribution to the coaching and creativity literature, one that couldn't have appeared before creativity coaching became a reality.

Creativity coaches are in the unique position of sharing exercises that they have used with clients and that they know work. Please enjoy the exercises in this book. I hope you'll think about using them with clients, and you may also find them personally useful.

Your Master Project List 1

Nadia Arbach

Exercise Purpose

To consolidate all of your creative projects into one master list.
To prioritize your creative projects based on excitement level.
To let go of creative projects you're no longer excited about.

 Exercise Description

Have you ever felt stuck, blocked, or overwhelmed because you have so many projects going on at once? When you have a significant number of projects (and ideas for new projects!) that need to be completed, you might feel like you just don't know where to start.

The Master Project List exercise will help you bring all of your projects together, rank them based on how excited you are about them, delete the ones that no longer excite you, and help you decide which ones will be your top priorities—so that you can get down to work, confident that you've got all your ideas in one place.

Step 1. List all of your projects. Get a blank sheet of paper and write down every single project you have in the works—or in your head as an idea. Walk around your creative workspace or your home and find all the projects you've been working on, that you've put aside for the moment, that you've bought the materials for but haven't started working on yet, and that you've planned in your head. Even if it's just a nebulous idea at the moment, give it a title and write it down anyway. The object of this step is to make sure that you haven't forgotten a single project or idea.

Step 2. Rate your projects by excitement level. Go through the list and give each project a rating on a scale of 1–5, where 1 means you're not excited about it at all, and 5 means you can't wait to work on it. You may never have thought of rating your projects by excitement level, but it's a true barometer of how you feel about your work. If you find that you have plenty of projects that rate lower on the scale, it will be an indicator that your work isn't in alignment with your values and desires. If you find that all your projects rate a 4 or 5, that's great! That means you've chosen work that truly lights you up and brings you joy.

Step 3. Cull your list. Take a look at all the projects that you rated a 1 or a 2, meaning that they hold little to no excitement for you. Cross all of these projects off the list!

You don't have to spend your precious time on projects that you don't love. If these are personal projects that have gone stale because too much time has passed or you just didn't enjoy the work, let them go—they've already served you by showing you that your true interests lie elsewhere. You have no further duty to complete them. Culling them from the list and removing them from your creative workspace will make room for what really excites you!

If these are work-based projects and you do have a duty to complete them even though you dislike them, go ahead and finish them up—but you may wish to examine whether you can be more selective about your work-based projects in the future, or whether you might switch directions so that your future projects contain more of what you love to do.

Step 4. Select your priority projects. From what remains of the list (all items that rated a 3, 4, or 5), select up to five projects to work on at once. Five is the maximum number I recommend to my clients—any more than that and things begin to get overwhelming again. If you know you don't enjoy working on several things at once, you may want to select only one or two projects from the list to make your priority for right now. Put a star next to each of the projects you decide to prioritize. Those are the projects you'll be working on right now, to the exclusion of everything else on the list.

Step 5. Revise your list as needed. Whenever you finish one of your starred priority projects, cross it off the list and add its star to any other project on your list to bring that project up to priority status. As you think of new ideas, add them onto the list and give them a rating of 1–5 for excitement level. And remember to go through the whole list every so often (I suggest about every two months) and examine your rating level for each project—sometimes our excitement will wane, or something will suddenly become much more compelling, so it's important to take note of these changes and act accordingly.

In Session or as Homework

Most clients will enjoy trying to remember all of the projects they have going on, so this is an exercise that can be begun during a session. Most clients will also be able to recognize right away that they're not as enamored of some of their projects as they thought they were.

However, they most likely won't remember everything that should go on the list, so the exercise will need to be finished as homework, with the client checking every area of their home/studio and their notes/plans to make sure that all projects have been captured in the list.

It may also be useful to follow up this exercise in future sessions by discussing how it feels to declutter or let go of certain projects. Projects that invoke a sense of duty—as well as sentimental projects—can be quite difficult to let go of, even when the client has given them a low rating for excitement level.

For Home Use

This is an excellent exercise to complete by yourself. Remember that your main aim is first to locate or remember *every* project and consolidate them all into one list. Don't worry about the number of projects! I've had clients with twenty projects and clients with over 200 projects. It doesn't matter how many you have or how many remain on the list. The point of this exercise is to uncover everything so that you can prioritize what you really love.

If you're an artist whose passion lies with one kind of art but your main financial income comes from a different kind of art, you may wish to create two separate Master Project Lists—one for personal/passion projects and one for income-generating projects. For the income-generating list, you may wish to replace "rating by excitement level" with a more conventional rating factor: you could rate by income potential or by deadline, depending on which is more relevant for you. However, I prefer to still rate these projects by excitement level, as this is an indicator of whether or not your creative work is in alignment with your desires.

 Client Results

When a client of mine tried this exercise, she began with over 200 projects and ideas that she wished to complete. Her level of overwhelm due to such a high number of projects was creating a huge amount of stress. It had also contributed to a buildup of clutter in her creative space because of the sheer amount of materials necessary for all these projects. At one point, she couldn't see the surfaces of her work tables and had many bags, boxes, and bins of project materials covering the floor.

Using the Master Project List method, she made a paper list of every project she had going on, gave the projects a rating based on excitement level, and then began culling the projects that gave her a low or negligible sense of excitement. Right away she was able to whittle down her list to a much more manageable number of projects, and the clutter began to disappear, too.

She found that because she's digitally inclined, recreating her list in a project management app called Trello allowed her to continue managing her projects much more easily. As a very prolific maker, she regularly completes several projects per week; using an app makes it easier for her to keep tabs on her quickly changing list.

 About Nadia Arbach

Nadia Arbach, The Creativity Coach, helps women transition their creative hobby into their Creative Dream Life. She uses her expertise as a Professional Declutterer to help her clients cut through any mindset issues that are no longer serving them, let go of their old identity as a hobbyist, and bring their creative work to the forefront of their life.

She is the author of four self-study online courses for creative women, and she runs a parallel business, Clear the Decks!, helping creative women declutter their creative workspaces.

You can contact Nadia via her websites at http://nadiaarbach.com and http://clearthedecks.co.uk.

Flipping on the Creative Switch Using the 4, 7, 8 Breathing Technique

2

Dwight McNair

Exercise Purpose

The purpose of this exercise is to empty the mind of all tension and extraneous thoughts and release any feelings of exhaustion and fatigue from your body, so you can fully use your imagination to actively create.

 Exercise Description

Most of us spend countless hours working and worrying about the things we have to do or have not done. This constant expenditure of energy and preoccupation with things we think we should do drains our energy reserves. These nonproductive thoughts deplete our creative energy and leave us feeling mentally and emotionally exhausted and unable to engage in our real creative work.

One extremely powerful way to escape this trap is to use a simple but efficient breathing technique called 4, 7, 8 breathing. This procedure is so simple and portable that it can be applied almost anywhere and under almost any set of circumstances.

Prepare your creative space. Make it a safe and sacred space for your creative freedom. If you can, close your eyes. This helps you relax and turns off all visual stimuli. However, closing your eyes is not necessary to achieve maximum results. Next, consciously breathe in and breathe out through the nose, as you would normally, for a few seconds.

Then breathe in deeply, silently counting to 4. Hold that breath, silently counting to 7. Exhale, slowly and continuously squeezing out all the air deep into your abdomen and pelvic floor to a silent count of 8. Return to normal breathing for a few seconds. Check in mindfully to assure that you're using the proper technique. Then repeat this procedure three more times consecutively. Four repetitions complete the cycle. Now that you have learned the technique, do four complete cycles whenever you need to enter your creative space.

This breathing technique relaxes and revitalizes you by sending oxygen to all of the cells of your body. It clears your mind and energizes your body. It takes you out of your linear/left-brain mode of thinking and allows you and your awareness to enter into your non-linear/right-brain mode. Said another way, it gets you out of your "head" (your thoughts) and puts you and your awareness into your body, opening you up to the land of infinite creative possibilities.

After completing this exercise, move immediately into your creative space and start your creative work.

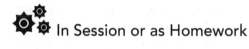 ## In Session or as Homework

This exercise can be used in a session to help clients release any feelings of fatigue, exhaustion, uneasiness, discomfort, or frustration that may be blocking some aspect of their creating process.

Ask your client to close their eyes as the coach gives the above directions. Ask them to close their mouth, place their hands on their belly, inhale through the nose, and allow the breath to expand their abdomen. Tell them to become more aware of their inner body. Tell them to inhale and hold their breath. Ask them to exhale slowly through the nose to a count of 8. Repeat this cycle at least three to four times. Then have the client scan their body to determine if they need to repeat the cycle again. When your client has practiced this procedure a few times and feels confident that they can apply this technique at home, give it as a homework assignment.

 ## For Home Use

This technique can easily be adapted to any creative's home use. First find yourself a quiet spot to apply this exercise. It can be extremely effective in any of the following situations: when you find yourself stymied after giving your best; if you are feeling apathetic or disinterested in beginning the creative task before you; if you are feeling jittery or agitated and there is creative work to do, flip the switch and use the 4, 7, 8 breathing technique to get yourself back on track and move into your creative zone.

 ## Client Results

I have used this exercise on myself with great results. Here's an example of how I used it on one long day. First, I was working rather intensely with a distraught singer who was feeling extremely insecure and unprepared for an important upcoming performance. I was encouraging her to focus on all the things that indicated that she was, in fact, very well prepared for her show the next night.

Next, I coached a client who was unable to communicate her need for punctuality and respect to certain male band members who didn't seem to understand that she, as a female, was entitled to the same courtesies and respect routinely given to the male members of their group.

Then I had two fairly routine voice lessons. By now it was two in the afternoon and I was finding myself mentally exhausted. But my work day was just beginning. I still had a two-hour songwriting session and a meeting with the head of a recreation center who wanted me to explain to the city's contracting specialist what my musical and creative vision was for the new teenage songwriting and music production program the city was asking me to develop. After that, I had a rehearsal looming for my upcoming performance for the homeless, which was happening in just two days.

As you can imagine, by the time I got to the rehearsal my mind was pure mush. I had absolutely no gas in my tank and no energy left. But, as this was my final rehearsal before the show and as there were a number of things that had to be polished and worked out, I had to both calm myself down and re-energize and ready myself for this crucial rehearsal.

I flipped on my creative switch by using several cycles of the 4, 7, 8 breathing technique. After applying this technique two times, I slowly began to feel my racing thoughts recede into the background. After the third application, my body began to feel lighter and less weighted down. I could feel myself recharging. But I was still feeling slow and unmotivated.

Then I applied the technique once more, inhaling more deeply this time and exhaling even more slowly and completely emptying my lungs for the last time. I paused . . . and then returned to normal breathing, allowing myself to gradually open my eyes and return to the present. I felt refreshed, revived, and ready to rehearse with a new sense of energy and vitality.

*

 About Dwight McNair

Dwight McNair is a singer/pianist/songwriter, vocal clinician, creativity coach, and author of *A Singer's Prayer and Meditation: A Spiritual Guide for Inspiration and Hope* and *25 Powerful Low or No Cost Things You Can Do NOW to Jump Start Your Singing or Instrumental Career*. He was an opening act for the legendary rhythm and blues singer Phyllis Hyman and has shared the stage with many notables, including jazz greats Barry Harris and Jon Hendricks of Lambert, Hendricks and Ross. He has performed nationally in the U.S. as well as in Europe, Africa, and Canada. He is the recipient of numerous awards, grants, and recognitions, among them a Fellowship to the Juilliard School of Music and the University of Ghana, where he did field studies in traditional African drumming, rhythm, and ritual. He currently operates a music studio in the Washington, DC area and is recording a new album to be released in 2020. He is also a certified yoga teacher and EFT (Emotional Freedom Technique) Practitioner. You can reach Dwight at dwightmcnair@icloud.com or dwightmcnair@aol.com or by phone at 202-486-3741.

Making Peace With Your Inner Critic

3

Jen Johnson

Exercise Purpose

To help creative people make peace with their inner critic and discover a sense of creative freedom.

 Exercise Description

Most creative people struggle at times with a harsh inner critic. Some methods recommend aggressive approaches to dealing with the inner critic, such as arguing with it, silencing it, or even banishing it. A mindfulness approach, however, recognizes that fighting against the inner critic often results in increasing its intensity, and thus, mindfulness takes the approach of making peace with it.

You can make peace with your inner critic by observing it from the perspective of an objective witness with an attitude of non-judgment and then practicing taking steps to activate an attitude of kindness and self-compassion. If you worry that you won't get anything done without being hard on yourself, it may help to know that being harsh toward yourself actually decreases creativity and productivity, because it activates a stress response.

When you are stressed, the more primitive areas of your brain that are concerned with basic survival are activated, which means that other areas of the brain are more deactivated, including the areas of the brain that relate to creativity. By contrast, being calm supports creativity and productivity, because when you are calm, the areas of your brain that relate to creativity are more activated.

One way to cultivate a state of calm is through writing meditation. This can be adapted to a number of specific situations or intentions, including making peace with the inner critic. When you notice the harsh voice of your inner critic, try taking 10–15 minutes to practice the following writing meditation:

1. Write a clear intention for this practice in your journal. For instance, "My intention is to make peace with my inner critic and access creative freedom."

2. The emphasis of this practice is on focusing your attention, calming your body and mind, and writing what you hear and feel. Try to let go of any concern about writing a well-crafted piece, and focus on getting the words down on paper, even if the sentence structure feels messy.

3. Take five deep breaths, breathing in to the count of four and breathing out to the count of six. Try to bring mindful, non-judgmental awareness to what is happening in this moment—practice objectively observing what is happening (which can help you feel calmer) rather than reacting to it (which can increase stress).

4. Notice what your inner critic is saying and how it leaves you feeling. Remind yourself that you don't have to believe what it says. Thoughts are just thoughts, and you don't have to believe or act on everything that you think. Try to observe your experience with an attitude of non-judgment and neutrality, listen to your thoughts, sensations, and feelings, and write what you hear.

5. Whatever you hear, just write that—"I hear my inner critic telling me that I'm an idiot, my work is awful, and I will never be good enough. I notice a sensation of tightness in my throat. I feel anxious." Try to continue to objectively observe what you hear as well as your response to it with an attitude of non-judgment. Write whatever comes into your awareness.

6. One of the most painful aspects of feeling at the mercy of your harsh inner critic is the belief that you're the only one who struggles with this negative inner voice and the belief that there must be something wrong with you. Take a moment to try to broaden your perspective by writing a few sentences to remind yourself that you are not alone in this very human experience. For instance, you might write something like, "A lot of people struggle with a harsh inner critic. It's part of being human." This step is intended to help you to further calm your mind and try to keep what's happening in perspective by perceiving what's happening as simply a shared experience rather than becoming entangled in the belief that something is wrong with you.

7. Now try to bring to mind an image or phrase that represents someone showing you unconditional love and kindness, and write about it. This someone can be a loved one, living or deceased, a pet, a spiritual being, or any other being. Examples that some of my clients have come up with include your dog kissing your face, your grandmother or other beloved person kissing you on the forehead, a loved one hugging you, sitting underneath the shade of a tree, or resting your head in the lap of a spiritual being. Now take a moment to notice how it feels to have this energy of love, kindness, and compassion directed toward you, and write a few sentences about that. In this step, we're actively choosing to rest the attention on receiving kindness and compassion and resting in the sense of calm that this can activate.

8. Take a few moments to reflect on this practice. When you feel ready, turn your attention back to your creative process. Repeat this practice as needed.

In Summary

1. When you become aware that your inner critic is activated, take a moment to practice writing meditation for making peace with your inner critic. Write a clear intention for your practice: "My intention is to make peace with my inner critic and access creative freedom."

2. Write what you observe—what you hear your inner critic saying to you and the sensations and feelings that this evokes.
3. Write a few sentences to remind yourself that you're not alone in this experience, that others struggle with this, too.
4. Write about being shown unconditional love and kindness from another being.
5. Turn your attention back to being creative.

 ## In Session or as Homework

Writing meditation for making peace with your inner critic can be used in session by guiding your client through each step of the writing meditation practice. You can offer the prompts verbally or in writing. Encourage your client to focus on listening to their thoughts, sensations, and feelings and writing those down without worrying about proper grammar or punctuation.

This practice can be offered as a homework assignment by writing down the steps of the writing meditation practice and inviting the client to write in response to each of the prompts.

 ## For Home Use

You can easily use writing meditation at home by following the steps to the practice, writing down the prompts, and writing in your journal or on a piece of paper in response to the meditation prompts. Try to remember to place your focus on using writing as a meditation practice and not on writing a well-crafted piece.

Client Results

When I first met with Susie, she told me that she had always loved writing. For years she had enjoyed writing in her journal about her experiences in nature. But when she tried to expand from journaling to writing essays, she felt creatively blocked. She felt as though her inner critic was in charge and was stopping her from writing anything at all. Susie had bought into believing the words of her inner critic—"You don't have anything interesting to say; nobody would ever publish your work; you'll never be good enough; your writing is boring and awful."

Prior to working with me, Susie had been trying to manage her inner critic by fighting with it, arguing against it, and attempting to banish it, but she said that this resulted in it increasing in volume, intensity, and frequency. Her inner critic simply became more insistent—"You're not really a writer, and you never will be. Stick with your day job. And stick to journaling so no one will have to read this mess."

Early on in our work together, I taught Susie the writing meditation practice. After practicing for a few weeks, she noticed that her inner critic became less intense and harsh, and she became less reactive to it. Within several more weeks, Susie began writing. We were then able to focus our time and attention during sessions toward learning additional writing meditation practices to help her write with greater consistency and ease. Within a relatively short period of time, Susie was writing on a regular basis and began writing essays. Several months later, one of her essays was accepted for publication in a literary journal. Susie continues to write and publish her work on a regular basis. She is now writing her first book.

**

 About Jen Johnson

Jen Johnson is a mindfulness and creativity coach and psychotherapist. She is a licensed professional counselor and board-certified coach and holds master's degrees in counseling and rehabilitation counseling and an MFA in interdisciplinary arts.

Jen teaches meditation and creativity for healing and creative freedom. She coaches people to develop a regular mindfulness meditation practice and integrate it into everyday life. Her areas of expertise include meditation for creativity and mind/body healing from illness and difficult times. Jen offers individual coaching and teaches online courses on meditation and creativity. You can visit her at meditatecreate.com or jenjohnson.com and contact her at jen@jenjohnson.com.

Creative Geometry

4

Francesca Aniballi

Exercise Purpose

The purpose of this exercise is to jumpstart a new creative project, or to get unstuck when you are already working on one. It is particularly suitable to writers, but it can also be used by creatives working in other mediums, as a refreshing way to overcome a stalemate, as it is quite versatile.

 Exercise Description

You will need some paper sheets or a notepad and colored pens. On each clean sheet, draw a big geometrical shape: first, a triangle, then a square, a rectangle, and finally a circle.

Contemplate each shape for a few moments, softening your focus: contemplation of geometrical figures stimulates the observer's mind and has been used in meditation for ages.

Then pick a colored pen intuitively. What words come to mind? Within each geometrical shape, jot down the first five words that come to your mind. Think of concrete objects and/or actions. Do not use abstract words.

When you have the words for each geometrical figure, use all of them as stepping stones or a roadmap to expand your project. Either write a short tale or make a sketch of the issues, themes, and solutions that come to you regarding the project at hand. Do not overthink the process. Just write quickly and let your imagination do the work.

 In Session or as Homework

The exercise can be used best in a one-to-one coaching session or by the creative at home. It can be amplified by adding colors, sketches, and/or doodles to the five words contained within each of the four geometrical figures, in order to provide extra layering, thus enriching the silt of your creative project. It can be used as a brainstorming tool or by your client to expand and/or reflect on his or her current creative project.

 For Home Use

At home, the exercise works very well with ambient music, conscious breathing, or progressive relaxation techniques that release stress. After 5–10 minutes of preliminary breathing or relaxation, pick up the sheets and pens and start the exercise.

It works best when done quickly and intuitively. You can also adapt the exercise to facilitate the incubation stage of the creative process through meditation, by associating specific natural qualities and elements to the geometrical figures.

You can look into various cosmologies, such as the Indian or Chinese ones, to be inspired, and you can also read the short seminal essay by the Russian artist Wassily Kandinsky, *On the Spiritual in Art*. For painters, it is quite possible to use the geometrical shapes as containers for specific micro-patterns, so that they build up a new personal alphabet or language to be explored later in their paintings.

Client Results

I have used this exercise primarily with creative writers, who produced short tales starting from the words they had jotted down. Some used these short pieces as springboards for longer stories, novellas, and even novels. Others found the exercise useful as a way to think about their current projects from new angles.

Storytellers can also benefit from this exercise, since it helps to build up narrative in layers and different scene frames through visual thinking. I also personally use this exercise when I am in need of a fresh concept or perspective.

As an example, take Frank, a writer who had written two short story collections. When he came to see me, he had decided that it was time for him to finally tackle a novel. However, he felt stuck and overwhelmed by the complexity of the task, as something in him refused to settle for a linear chapter outline.

We interacted online through Skype. I watched him draw each of the geometrical shapes meticulously, with utter precision and focus. First the triangle, then the square, then the rectangle, and finally the circle. The latter was slightly tilted to the left. As he looked, he let himself be absorbed within the geometrical figures. Then, slowly, he picked a red pen for the triangle.

"The triangle is very active," he said. I nodded, as a way of encouraging him to explore his own associations further. He scribbled down five words: fireworks, burst, firefly, run, and summer. He went through the same process again: yellow pen for the square, green for the rectangle, blue for the circle. He came up with fifteen additional words. When he finished, I invited him to sip some water from the glass on his desk.

"What's next?" he said.

"Now connect your twenty words in a short tale."

He buckled down to write for 30 minutes. His hand moved in sprints across the page, a sardonic smile on his lips. I could see from his bent-over position that he had let go of his own reservations and preconceptions about the exercise. When the allotted time was over, he read what he had written.

"Good God! Where does this stuff come from?" he said at last, wide-eyed.

I suggested that he should continue by using the nested approach: that is, repeating the previous process whenever, as he worked on his tale, he felt he needed to know more, thus expanding the weft of his narrative. In fact, that was to be his homework over the following two weeks, until our next session.

When we met again, he sat in front of his computer screen holding a paper stack: clearly, he had made good progress. Over the following month, by using this method, he wrote the "zero draft," a sprawling draft where you just put on paper everything that comes up, without censoring yourself, including reflections, fragments, etc. Certainly, it was a messy draft, but it proved an excellent start, and Frank was well on his was to writing his first novel.

**

 ## About Francesca Aniballi

Francesca Aniballi is an Artbundance coach, art therapist, and creative facilitator based in Italy, not far from Rome. She works both in person and online with individuals and groups, using creative processes and activities as catalysts for clients' full self-expression and creative work. She also is a teacher and cultivated her passion for literature and anthropology through postgraduate studies and research. She enjoys reading in several genres, practices creative writing and therapeutic writing under the pen name Frances Fay, as well as intuitive drawing, painting, and collage. You can learn more about her and her work by visiting her website and contacting her at:

fb.me/FrancesCreativeCoachingandContent
m.me/FrancesCreativeCoachingandContent
francesca.aniballi@gmail.com
www.francesfay.it

A Birthday Present for the Muse

5

Elise V. Allan

Exercise Purpose

When your creative work needs new life breathed into it, this exercise will enable you to access your subconscious inspiration through visualizing resources that can open up exciting new possibilities.

 Exercise Description

This guided visualization will take less than 10 minutes, followed by time for reflection and planning.

Begin by connecting your feet to the ground beneath you, acknowledging that your resources come from our planet and that you're aiming to bring your ideas down to Earth.

Sit with a straight back, both feet flat on the floor, hands separated. Shut your eyes, or if you prefer, look down, keeping your gaze relaxed and unfocused. Bring your attention to where your feet contact the ground, sensing the aliveness of the earth beneath you, and holding the awareness that it has already provided all that has enabled you to survive.

If you can, develop a sense of your feet having a warm relationship with the ground. Gently notice how you are breathing in Earth's atmosphere, then take time to exhale slowly out of your mouth; repeat a few times until you feel relaxed.

When you're ready, visualize going to a place where you can create—perhaps your existing studio, perhaps an imagined space. You will find a surprise there—maybe in an envelope or a parcel, or possibly the space itself will have been transformed. This is a birthday present for your Muse—exactly what your Muse wants and your creative heart's desire. Explore the gift or gifts—and the feelings around them. Take time to enjoy whatever you find.

Allow yourself time to return slowly to the here and now, holding a sense of relaxation and the memories of the visualization. Open your eyes and write down what you experienced before beginning to reflect on what you want to manifest.

In Session or as Homework

This visualization works well in a group or read out loud to a client in a one-to-one session.

Before starting this exercise, the coach would suggest to the group or to the individual to mull over what feels stuck or stale. Maybe your creative time or space might lack rhythm. Or you might feel that your art practice already has rhythm and a bit of a groove, but that the groove is in danger of becoming a rut. The aim is to reignite your enthusiasm.

The coach or facilitator would read out the instructions while picking up from the client or the group a sense of how long to allow between sentences, so as to relax everyone. After the visualization, verbal feedback is shared; the group would write down their thoughts and recollections before speaking.

The feedback sparks questions around what resources are needed in order to put inspiration into action—new skills, adaptation of old skills, or formal learning. It might be time, space, materials, money, or reorganization of resources—materials or workspace. There might be choices to be made about letting something go to allow space for the new. Clients might identify a major change that involves long-term planning, a smaller project they can put into action immediately, or a series of small regular changes.

Committing to that next action, and timetabling it, completes the exercise. It might be a day to begin researching costs or possibilities, or it might be something as simple as reorganizing a corner of the studio. Group participants might buddy up and set a date to report to one another.

 ## For Home Use

If you are working alone on the exercise, it can be helpful to record yourself reading the instructions out loud, leaving approximately 20 seconds between each sentence in the introductory paragraph, and about 5 minutes at the end before gently announcing that the visualization is over.

Afterwards you would reflect in writing on the value of what you've visualized. Allow yourself to consider what you would do if your resources were limitless, and once you're clear about what you'd like in an ideal world, begin to consider realistic alternatives, scaling down the plans or allowing a long enough time scale for the ideal.

Put a date in your diary. For a small project, the date would represent the date for putting that project into action. For a big project, the date would be more for planning and researching, costing, or checking availability. Choose a date that feels right for you, finding the happy spot between over-pressurizing yourself and procrastination.

Client Results

When I led this visualization with a group, Laura, a well-known illustrator of children's books who makes meticulously detailed watercolors, had been feeling exhausted by the pressure to meet one deadline after another.

She visualized herself as an undergraduate art student making large gestural paintings. She knew that she was very lucky to be earning a living as an illustrator, and with dependents to care for, she didn't feel that she could apply for a degree course in fine arts for at least four years. But the exercise caused her to rethink her situation, and a month later she told us that she'd started a class, one morning a week, where she was learning to paint loosely and freely—and she was sparkling! She'd been able to cut back on some of the less lucrative but labor-intensive commissions and, since then, has booked herself into several additional short painting courses.

Marie, an established designer, felt overwhelmed by her extremely cluttered studio. Always busy with commissions, she had less time than she liked to declutter or to generate new ideas. She'd been working on clearing unwanted clutter from her studio for 10 minutes a day for some time. In the exercise, she visualized a glass table, in a clear space, in the middle of her studio where she could make monotypes. Acting on this was straightforward—she began to focus her daily decluttering sessions on this area and created a space where she's now making monotypes, which are generating a new stream of ideas.

Some visualizations will take time to bear fruit. Luke, a painter, was surprised: he saw himself entering an empty dance studio. He talked about his desire to dance and his longing for an empty space, and decided to research the costs of renting a dance studio. He's currently exploring those possibilities, and even though they haven't borne fruit yet, he is sure that he is on to something.

I had a similar vision about twelve years ago when my painting practice was at an impasse. I dreamt of studying Butoh, a Japanese underground dance movement. Online searches led only to unrealistic options. Months passed, and then I had a chance conversation with a friend about unlived dreams. Synchronicity occurred—one week later he told me of a Butoh class to be held in my city—the first ever. It completely transformed and regenerated my painting practice within a year.

** **

 **About Elise V. Allan**

Elise V. Allan has observed—as a practicing painter, an accredited creativity coach, and a part-time lecturer—that the biggest obstacles in our creative lives are often caused by where we've positioned ourselves. We get in the way of our own light. Sometimes the smallest of shifts allows the light back in. And sometimes it takes sustained care to gently woo our Muses back. Elise coaches by email, in person, or by Zoom, working one-to-one and with groups, short-term or long-term. You can contact her at:

www.elisevallan-creativitycoaching.co.uk

or on Facebook:

@EliseVAllancreativitycoaching

Her paintings are at www.elisevallan.com.

Thresholds

6

Embracing and Utilizing Liminality

Litza Bixler

Exercise Purpose

To teach the idea of "liminality."

What is liminality? The concept of *liminality* was developed by anthropologist Victor Turner as a means of describing the middle stage of a rite of passage. A *liminal space* is the space in between, a sort of limbo. The word comes from *limen*, meaning "threshold."

Doorways, windows, portals, wormholes, rabbit holes, and caves are all physical thresholds. They are the links between worlds that the hero must pass through in order to arrive at a new symbolic life.

This exercise acknowledges that people often find themselves in between projects, ideas, careers, and life stages. In a culture that emphasizes productivity and forward momentum, it can be challenging to embrace these periods. However, the "in-between" can be an open, fertile space to explore potential ideas and paths forward.

 Exercise Description

This exercise is an experiential, embodied process that can be done at home, in a coaching session, or in a workshop. The exercise is divided into two parts, and each part is distinct. They can be done separately or together.

Part One: It's Okay to Be In Between

Now is the time to embrace blue-sky thinking and to revel in potential.

1. Choose a doorway: at home or in a private space at work.
2. Stand in the doorway and close your eyes. Breathe deeply. Take a moment to concentrate on your breathing and to embrace the sensation of being on the threshold.
3. You are not in one room or another. You could turn around and go back to the room you just left, or you could choose to step forward into a new room. Acknowledge the pressure to choose, to step forward or back, and let that go.

Part Two: Stepping Over the Threshold

Now is the time to decide what to work on next. Where to go. And who to be.

At some point, the time of transition ends. Alice lands at the bottom of the rabbit hole. The husband carries the wife over the threshold. The mother gives birth. The teenager becomes an adult.

This part of the exercise uses the wisdom of the body to access the client's intuition about which idea, which project, or which life path is right for him or her at this time. Use it when the client or participant is ready to move out of *liminality* towards something new.

1. Find a doorway and stand on the threshold. Close your eyes and focus on your breathing.
2. Visualize a space in front of you. It could be an internal space, like a room, or an external one, like a garden. What does it look like? What does it feel like? Is it warm, cool, or breezy? What color is it? Are there objects or living things in it? What are they?
3. Now imagine that this space is on a rotating platform. Count backwards from ten (aloud, if you can). When you arrive at zero, the platform stops and delivers a new space. Repeat step three for each new space, up to a maximum of four. Next, intuitively assign a project, an idea, or a new path to each. Then visualize them again.
4. Now breathe in and exhale. On the exhale, the rotating platform stops. After each rotation, notice whether you feel a physical pull towards any of the imagined spaces. Is the sensation strong enough to pull you over the threshold and into one of these spaces? If so, allow yourself to literally walk over the threshold.

 ## In Session or as Homework

It's useful to explore the concept of liminality before beginning the exercise. The coach then guides the client through the process as outlined previously. If the coach is trained in hypnotherapy, it is useful to bring the client into a light trance during the breathing work. This helps them to access their visualization skills.

 ## For Home Use

Clients can guide themselves through the process, or print out the instructions and have another person do it. The key is to utilize the physical experience of standing in a threshold.

Variations: Encourage participants to explore other types of thresholds as well: an archway, a beach, a driveway, the gate into a garden, or the edge of a forest, for example.

Client Results

I've used this exercise myself and with a variety of clients. It's useful for people who find themselves at a crossroads or at a point of transition.

Note that clients can move through these imagined spaces fluidly. For instance, they might choose to travel across the threshold and back into a space they've previously inhabited.

"Just because I created a new path in the future, doesn't mean I have to leave the present behind," explained Claire, a dancer. "Maybe I could just add to my world and make it bigger, rather than deduct what I have already created."

Stuart, an engineer, noted that he felt a tug backwards, towards the space that represented his current job. This led him to question whether he really wanted to leave. He then explored ways he could learn new skills while remaining in his present position.

In previous versions of this exercise, I used an image of a carousel during the meditation. Sometimes clients became distracted by images of carousels, cotton candy, and amusement parks, so I switched to the more neutral image of a rotating platform. It's important to be conscious of the images used in the visualization, since these images can push the client towards a particular set of symbols and meanings.

* *

 About Litza Bixler

Litza Bixler is a creative polymath with a wealth of experience across a wide range of art forms, including film, fine art, choreography, and writing. She is a certified Kaizen-Muse Creativity Coach, with additional certificates in counseling and hypnotherapy. She also has a master's degree in Dance Anthropology, with additional training in a broad range of dance and somatic techniques.

Litza's creative journey has been full of twists and turns, ups and downs, playfulness and laughter, interesting characters, and of course a few dark nights of the soul. She set up Compasso Coaching to help others discover their own *true north* and navigate their journey with compassion, creativity, and courage. Through deep listening, open questions, and experiential exercises, she encourages others to become active participants in their stories. Visit Litza at www.compassocoaching.com or www.litzabixler.com.

Invoking Your Name Like a Miracle Mantra

7

Aneesah Wilhelmstätter

Exercise Purpose

To help creatives prime themselves for new possibilities through envisioning, embracing, and embodying their Greatest Possible Selves (GPS) rather than remaining Prisoners of the Past.

 Exercise Description

Invoking Your Name Like a Miracle Mantra is a self-valuing tool designed to help creatives tap into their personalities, upgrade their character, strengthen their identities, and honor their unlimited creative potential.

By ceremonially investing our names with cherished values, beliefs, and principles that evoke a vision of a Greatest Possible Self (GPS), we generate a meaning-rich miracle mantra that empowers us to face and overcome challenges in a centered and connected way.

Feeling the supportive presence of an inner GPS, while holding our intentions front and center, helps us experience ourselves differently and look to new possibilities instead of choosing from the past.

How much more likely are you to feel driven to meet the blank canvas/page, when your attitude favors approach rather than avoidance? How much more likely are you to create authentically when you prize your individuality more than you need the approval or fear the judgment of others? How much more likely are you to complete your work when you choose to take the bad with the good instead of refusing to accept reality?

What can a person do to surpass any and even all of these challenges and come out all the stronger for it? It is my belief that this tool gives creatives the support they need to roll with possibility instead of renouncing their potential—and not just when our sole hope of resolution demands the divine intervention of a miracle! What if your name could be a personal direct dial-in to a miracle-on-demand that allows you to fulfill your unlimited creative potential?

In Session or as Homework

Lead your creative client into this exercise with the provocative question: "What if it were possible for you to be the best possible version of yourself? What would you do if you knew that you had nothing to lose and everything to gain by going after what you want?"

Discuss how creating a powered-up name (an acroname) can help them see themselves differently, reframe the way they look at the world, and transform their lives. Your client then kickstarts this four-step process by selecting a resonant-feeling name, one that sparks the feeling or spirit of the "supernatural and sacred."

1. With a deep centering breath, the client practices "calling on" their chosen name, preferably out loud, with three repetitions each time until it feels natural, inviting a sense of release and relaxation.
2. The designated name is next captured onto separate sheets of paper, by anchoring each letter in a circle (or any other shape) of its own.
3. In a light-hearted brainstorming session, your client ceremoniously "invokes the miracle" with the prompt: "What if a miracle has happened and I am doing what needs to be done? What do I see myself doing differently?" Rays of possibility can now be "drawn on," using treasured values, principles, and character qualities, e.g., "A—awaken." Creatives are encouraged to take direct aim at countering self-limiting attitudes, habits, and challenges of their personality.
4. The *acroname* takes final shape when your client intuitively assigns a single resonant affirmation, for example, "I awaken to freedom," to each of the composite characters. This can be done on a single page. In a future session, or as homework, supporting statements can be added to continue this self-conversation and expand this manifesto and this vision of a more resourceful and heroically authentic self.

Your client can now apply this powerful tool to a specific challenge by naming the challenge to be met and imagining invoking their name while meeting the encounter. This might be practiced in session, to be completed as homework, with the evocative question: "What would my GPS do?" The question might be repeated, using their own name instead of "my GPS." This is followed by the miracle mantra: "[*client's acroname*], I need a miracle!" With repeated practice, your client will develop their own idiosyncratic ways of invoking their "name."

This checking in can come in the shape of a verbal or written after-action reflection and can include an added-on "gratitude self-harmonizing" prompt. This would involve the completion of a prompt referencing the value that was resourced, for example: "I want to thank me . . . for courageously awakening to my freedom to do things differently."

 For Home Use

I invite you to give yourself the gift of time for this exercise (maybe 15 minutes) to engage the possibility that you too can get to your creative work in new ways. Allow yourself to surrender to the process by embracing a playful attitude, as you bravely call to mind your intention to step in the direction of "Yes." Let the miracle come to you by open-heartedly pondering this miracle question: "What if a miracle has happened and I am doing what needs to be done, what can I see myself doing differently?"

Draw a circle (or any other shape) to anchor any *one* letter of your name. Gently deepen your experience by contemplating the question: "What would GPS do?"

To start getting an intuitive sense of your cherished values and principles and the character qualities that might help you most, ceremonially invoke the mantra: "[*your acroname*], I need a miracle!"

Let this guide you as you create the rays of your sun using several aspirational affirmations (e.g., "I awaken to freedom"). Select the most resonant-feeling affirmation. "Soak it in" by breathing in for a count of 5 seconds and then out for a count of 5 seconds, viscerally sensing part of the affirmation on the inhale and part on the exhale.

Putting pen to paper, complete the prompt: "The challenge I intend to meet is . . .", followed by a description of the challenge. With your affirmation in mind, take a moment to reflect on how this value you have chosen might help you meet the encounter in a new, more resourceful way. Write down any insights and inspired actions that come to mind. My clients find it uplifting to honor this sense of support with a self-gratitude ritual: "My GPS is thanking me for . . ." (e.g., awakening to freedom).

 ## Client Results

My name felt "tired" from a lifetime of traumatic misuse, which included expectations of submission to a sibling's bullying because living up to my name meant that I had to be "the affectionate one."

In my late forties, I heroically stood up to a narcissistic spouse's "name-calling." When my creativity coach invited me to use my name as a mantra, I was primed to bring healing, resolve, and even pride to my name.

Initially, my acroname helped reduce anxiety and grow much-needed self-trust. Fast forward seven years later, and my daily "go-to" ritual is still rewarding me in exciting and unexpected ways as I continue to discover newer, more resourceful, and enriching ways to tap into its infinitely miraculous blessings.

David, an author, shared: "One morning, while repeating my miracle mantra: 'What would David do?' I found myself face-to-face with an unlikable image of myself in my bathroom mirror. An epiphany struck me like a bolt of lightning! I suddenly saw clearly how my excuses were defining and diminishing my life. This rude awakening was, believe it or not, uplifting and inspiring.

"Feeling driven, I directed myself to address my three most undermining habits: I needed to switch out my appetite for blaming others with an appetite for genuine accountability; I needed to vow 'permission to write freely'; and I needed my new perfection to be impeccable honesty! Several days of experimentation reaped the acroname: 'Daring Alchemists Vow Impeccable Devotion!'

"Now, one year on, thanks to my daily ritual of naming my intentions, invoking my name, and embracing a sense of feeling accompanied, I have my completed book in my hands. I also love the person I am becoming, the person who is present and willing to notice my thoughts and feelings, and who is prepared to challenge and change them with self-compassion. Writing has become a more centered and creative experience, and I feel more authentically connected to my work than ever before."

** **

About Aneesah Wilhelmstätter

Aneesah Wilhelmstätter is a self-taught artist, creativity and life purpose coach, writer, and workshop facilitator. Her life as an expat in the Netherlands, Paris, and London sparked a passion for creative change and transforming herself through her own Hero's Journey. Creator of the Tarot of Experience and author of several books, including *Passion to Performance*, *The Expat's Way*, and *The Thankful Way Journal*, Aneesah worked in the fields of mental health and as a clinical social worker before founding Creative Change Coaching in 2001. Visit Aneesah at:

https://creativechangecoaching.wordpress.com/

and learn about her miracle rituals and ceremonies at https://miracleroutines.home.blog/

Discomfort as Creative Fuel   8

Gina Edwards

Exercise Purpose

This exercise helps creatives distinguish between the discomforts that hold us back and those that nourish our growth and expansion. Knowing the difference allows us to use discomfort to regain momentum on stalled projects or goals. Practiced over time, it can teach us how to use discomfort to reignite the passion for our creative dreams.

 Exercise Description

Being a thriving creative means continuously learning, growing, and expanding. Naturally, that requires pushing ourselves into unfamiliar territory, often dealing with people we don't know, having to say things we've never said and do things we've never done. Creative growth also means experiencing emotions and thoughts that we're unaccustomed to and that might even feel scary. While humans prefer to gravitate toward pleasure, ease, and safety, creatives cannot flourish unless we extend ourselves outside our comfort zones.

"Discomfort as Creative Fuel" can help you distinguish between the discomforts that stifle you and the ones that are natural effects of extending yourself to become the creative person you long to be. Understanding discomfort as part of the creative process can transform it from something that extinguishes your creative passion into something that ignites it.

This exercise combines breath work and visualization with journaling. Although it's described here for writers, it's useful for all creative types. A coach can guide a group or individual client through the exercise and/or you can practice it on your own. Paper, pen or pencil, and a comfortable place to sit are all that's needed. If you're doing this at home, the breath work could be done lying down rather than sitting.

In Session or as Homework

Begin by closing your eyes and looking to your "third eye," toward the middle of your forehead. This is a center point for intuition, manifesting, and perception of both our inner and outer worlds. Don't strain or cross your eyes; simply turn your attention gently toward this area between your eyebrows.

Now take three to five breaths to calm and center yourself. Inhale deeply through your nose and exhale slowly and fully through your mouth, relaxing into each breath, releasing any tensions in your body. In a group situation, a coach can gently direct participants through each cycle of breath and relaxation.

When you're fully relaxed, consider an activity or an action that's come up for you recently, something you've had on your mind to do but have not attempted. For example, it might be completing that disturbing scene in your novel, decluttering your writing space, or accepting an invitation to talk to a book club. It can be anything, big or small, that you've resisted.

Once you've chosen an activity to focus on, hold it in your mind for several minutes as you continue to gaze, with eyes closed, toward your third eye. Visualize how it would feel to actually do the activity. What would you be thinking and feeling while doing it? Consider the possible outcome of this activity. What would you be thinking and feeling once the activity is actualized or complete? Stay with your visualization for 3–4 minutes.

Now, gradually open your eyes and reach for your journal or notebook. First, jot down the activity you chose to focus on. Then, using the following prompts, record the thoughts and feelings you inventoried while you were holding that activity and its outcome in your mind.

+ When I think about doing (the activity), I . . .
+ When I visualize (the activity) as done or complete, I . . .

You can free-write or follow these prompts, whichever feels right for you. As an example, here is a portion of what one client wrote: "When I think about speaking to a book club, I wonder why anyone would want to hear me talk about my book. I get terribly nervous in front of a group and my hands get sweaty. Sometimes I feel like I'll faint. I think I'm going to make a fool of myself. I'd like to accept their invitation—the organizer said they loved my book—but I also want to go hide under a rock."

Repeat the two prompts for your own activity and go deeper each time. Foremost, be honest with yourself about your thoughts and feelings. Fill at least one page and up to two pages if time allows.

When you've finished writing or when time is up, close your eyes and take three long, cleansing breaths to release any residual tension. Open your eyes to review what you've written, looking for any words or phrases that could relate to a state of discomfort, words and phrases like *nervous, humiliated, not worthy, depressed, afraid, tired, lazy, not smart enough, not talented enough, not (whatever) enough*. In our example, the writer's discomforts showed up in her wonderment that anyone would want to hear her talk about her book, and were described in the following ways: "I get nervous, my hands get sweaty, I feel like I'll faint, I feel like I'll make a fool of myself, and I want to go hide."

What words and phrases that represent discomfort have you used in your written piece? Underline them. Now circle the one word or phrase that resonates most strongly for you in this moment. Focusing on this, ask yourself the following questions:

1. When I consider (the activity), why do I feel or think (insert word/phrase)?
2. Is this discomfort presenting itself because doing or completing (the activity) would put me outside my comfort zone?
3. Would doing or completing (the activity) move me closer to my goal(s) or dreams?
4. Once (the activity) is complete, would I feel a sense of accomplishment or satisfaction?

Respond honestly, going as deeply as you can. Then pick another discomfort and repeat the question-answer process.

These questions are intended to separate out the two types of discomfort. The first variety is the result of a churning mind that offers up beliefs, opinions, or self-judgments that cannot be substantiated by evidence—such as "I'll make a fool of myself," "Why would anyone care about my book?" and "Why would anyone want to hear me talk about it?" This type of discomfort is associated with beating yourself up and is to be avoided.

The second type of discomfort is an effect of reaching toward your dreams and doing what you need to do to support your creative life. It comes from anticipating and entering into new or unfamiliar territory—for example, the nervousness that might accompany speaking to a group such as a book club. This discomfort is borne out of extending yourself to grow and expand. It should be expected and embraced as a natural part of the creative life.

Look back at your writing and your responses to these questions. Can you distinguish between the discomforts that serve you and those that do not?

 ## For Home Use

These instructions work beautifully for home use, either for you as the coach to use yourself or for clients to use.

 ## Client Results

I originally developed this exercise for myself after admitting a resistance to completing my novel. I needed a tool to distinguish between the discomforts that serve me and those that do not. Using the four questions, I examined the different varieties of fear, anxiety, and overwhelm I sometimes feel in the writing process.

Here is one set of my responses related to the discomfort of feeling anxious:

1. When I think about finishing my book, I feel anxious because I'm afraid someone (anyone, doesn't matter who!) won't like my writing once it's published.
2. The discomfort of being judged is absolutely outside my comfort zone. Who doesn't want to be loved?!
3. Completing my book would put me one step closer to being a published novelist.
4. I can easily visualize (and feel) how proud I'll be once my novel is published. It will give me a deep sense of accomplishment.

Repeating the exercise over time, focusing on a different discomfort each time, this question-response process has taught me to recognize the useful discomforts, to embrace them as part of the process, and to see them as motivation for reaching for my dreams.

I also use this exercise with clients who, despite being clear about their goals and dreams, feel stuck or overwhelmed. When resistance or inaction are setting in, the discomforts that stifle creativity are usually beginning to take hold, and this is the perfect time to practice this exercise.

You can use this exercise for any activity you've resisted. Practiced over time, it can help you direct the discomfort you experience toward being fuel for your creative dreams.

**

 ## About Gina Edwards

Gina Edwards is a retreat leader, a certified creativity coach, and a book editor. She is also a writer, so she's intimately familiar with the challenges and elation that come with being one. She supports all writers—published and aspiring—who want to write as an act of courageous and necessary self-expression. Walking the writer's path hand-in-hand with her clients and students, she helps them establish a writing practice and define a creative life on their own terms. You can connect with Gina at www.AroundTheWritersTable.com.

Seeing Is Believing

9

Liz Verna

Exercise Purpose

To tease out subconscious beliefs that block or sabotage creative energy.

 Exercise Description

Creatives are encouraged to write freely, uncensored, and in a stream-of-consciousness way about a particular challenge and their feelings about it for a finite period of time, not more than 5 or 10 minutes. All questions, accusations, and fears are welcomed onto the page. Then they are to read over their writing reflectively, isolating statements that appear as facts and circling them.

These "facts" are indicators, undercover arrows pointing at beliefs created by past events and hidden away from the cool surface of conscious awareness. Each of these statements is to be considered separately as the client asks: "What must I believe for this to be true?" Answers may be written in list form beneath, leaving room for scrutiny and confrontation.

For instance, the thought "I'm lazy" might be the frustrated sentiment of a procrastinator. But is that true? To challenge this belief, examples of *un*-lazy behavior could be listed. For example, a creative who loves to hike and who does it often is not lazy, but perhaps feels lethargic in the face of an impending deadline. This makes fear the real culprit, not a proclivity for sitting on the couch.

Perhaps "I'm lazy" is illuminating spots where a creative person needs to reassess his or her intention or ignite passion, or indicates a spot where practical help like bookkeeping, editing, advertising, etc. might be needed. "I'm lazy" derails a person's plans and projects, but if it's replaced with "I get tired when I'm stressed out, so I will allow for extra rest and structure my work time accordingly," that sentiment rids the creative of judgment, offers a chance for needed support, and replaces the dysfunctional belief with neutral reality plus actionable steps.

 In Session or as Homework

In session, this exercise can be used as a battering ram for a particularly stubborn block that is held in place in so tangled a way, via all sorts of defense mechanisms, that it can be near impossible to spot. In the moment, turning up the volume on a creative's self-talk by writing it down in a barebones list of "facts" makes his or her beliefs conscious, beliefs that drive every thought, feeling, and action the creative takes.

Encourage the creative to question the validity of their thoughts and to literally cross out the negative talk and write truer statements in their place, capping it by creating positive affirmations from these new, positive spins off the dysfunctional relics. Clients could write the affirmations a few times and copy them into future writing pages to be found in moments of need. Taking actionable steps towards combating sabotaging thoughts that inhibit their creative output is energizing and invigorating, and from this new space suggest a revisit to their current challenge.

You can wonder aloud if even one small step could be attempted—another paint stroke or another sentence written or a small plan created—if only to feel the lightness and shift of the dismantled block. As you move through your session, any other stumbles or issues the client experiences can be jotted down to be used as homework. Then, away from the moment of crisis, a calmer evaluation is possible. Outfitting clients with this tool to capture and analyze unconscious thoughts helps them to create a new relationship with their creativity and enables them to see the birthplace of a block rather than feel victim to it.

 ## For Home Use

This exercise is especially useful in the moment of block or frustration, but for home use I recommend the addition of a timer. Writing about anxiety-producing topics can often pull the writer down into greater feelings of rage and self-doubt, so imposing a finite amount of energy, between 5 and 10 minutes, can prevent this. The moment of reflection afterwards further grounds the creative into the present moment, where strengths and abilities are the focus, not the problems or hurdles.

Adding this exercise to any daily practice helps train the creative to question his or her blocks and to look for the cracks in the foundation rather than simply being crushed under the weight of forces that appear uncontrollable. It brings attention to the quiet messages muttering under the surface, and writing these down when noticed in a running tab of prompts builds muscles of inner connection, especially when a creative might feel abandoned or trampled by their creative drive and isolated by the solitary endeavors of creating. This exercise is a reminder that no one truly understands the internal struggles of creatives like they do, and writing can help access their inner guru.

 ## Client Results

As a therapist and coach setting up a practice, I have confronted overwhelming doubts and fears every step of the way, and I've found this exercise to be a powerfully grounding tool for reality-testing.

Am I really the worst writer who has ever lived or do I merely need an editor? Am I really incompetent or have I fallen down a rabbit hole of frustration and self-pity? I have used this exercise when I see that I am dragging or giving in to complacency, and it's especially effective if I use it objectively as data.

Most recently my frustrations about money, specifically a lack thereof, caused enough internal chaos that I took to my notebook. "Why Can't I Make Money?" shouted from the top of the page, and then underneath it I wrote, "Is that true? Am I not capable?" Amid the complaints ("Other people make money, why can't I?"), observations ("I thought doing what you loved and working hard brought money, what gives?"), and remembrances of salaries past ("I worked at some tough jobs and made good money") poked the persistent head of my deeply held belief ("I don't know what I'm worth") and the shameful, even bigger secret ("I don't feel worthy of money unless it's validated by someone else signing the check").

I should mention that sometimes the fruits of this exercise taste very bitter in the moment. This belief no doubt has some traumatic memories attached to it. Maybe my wonderfully warm, generous father gave me the message that good girls demurely accept gifts rather than aggressively attain their own. The origin of the belief could be explored and healed in therapy, although such work is not necessarily required to move past it. Once it became conscious, it appeared on my radar as something I could intentionally deconstruct and dismantle.

I have found this exercise helpful in developing my practical, business brain that looks only for solutions (like listing past successes, creating positive affirmations about my abilities, taking a business class, interviewing those I admire and asking their advice, etc.) without my having to take it personally. This felt empowering and changed "I'm not making money" to "I'm not making money *yet*" to "I'm buying a villa in Tuscany with all my extra money."

Judgment and fear are heavy bags to carry, and ambitious goals require lightness and aerodynamic fluidity if they are to be achieved. If I'm feeling lost writing a large project, it is simply more practical and pragmatic to combat the voice in my head that says "I'm not good enough" with "I need another set of eyes to read this." It keeps heavy self-judgment from crushing me and provides direction and tangible tools, but best of all it gives me the fuel to keep going, to not let ethereal insecurities win the day.

**

 **About Liz Verna**

Liz Verna is a licensed creative arts therapist and coach who uses writing as a way to channel creative energy and harness it to clear the path to artistic flow and productivity. She has written for more than forty years and, in that time, she has come to depend on her writing to clarify her own subconscious impulses and transform them into conscious intentions and goals. She has worked in broadcast media, education, customer service, and mental health using creativity and communication as her foundation for connection, which she now helps clients to channel in their own lives. Contact Liz Verna at www.lizverna.com.

Intention, Action, Reflection   **10**

Vinita Joseph

Exercise Purpose

This exercise helps us become more skilled at following through on our intentions. It also promotes an attitude of curiosity rather than self-judgment when things don't turn out quite as we had planned.

 Exercise Description

The exercise has three steps: (1) we form an *intention* to act; (2) we perform the intended *action*; (3) we *reflect* on what we have just done. It almost sounds too simple, but usually we do things in our old, habitual ways and, unsurprisingly, when we do the same things, we get the same results. Intention, Action, Reflection is an intervention that helps us to become conscious of the gap between our intentions and what we actually end up doing and, as importantly, to learn from it.

As creatives, we have big ambitions: we want to write novels, compose symphonies, film documentaries, and so on. Such projects consist of hundreds of actions, and it's easy to feel overwhelmed, so I spend a good deal of time with my clients organizing their work into clearly defined, manageable tasks. Clear goals enable us to set clear *intentions*.

The second step is attempting the *action*. I suggest that clients think of themselves as being in a laboratory during this stage, with the action as the experiment.

Once the action has been completed (or half-done or abandoned), the third and critical step is to *reflect* on what happened. Rather than thinking in terms of performance—did I do what I set out to do?—I encourage clients to see the attempt as an opportunity to learn. This is particularly important for creatives because tolerating uncertainty and taking risks are essential if we are to produce our best work.

When Thomas Edison was inventing the light bulb, he said: "I haven't failed. I've just found 10,000 ways that won't work." Hopefully it won't take us 10,000 attempts before we succeed, but Edison's attitude is worth emulating. Intention, Action, Reflection promotes this kind of flexible, curious mindset.

 In Session or as Homework

A novelist may, for example, decide to work on the scene in which Mary confronts Frank about why he comes home late every Thursday evening. We refine the goal further when I ask her how long she plans to spend on the task (or about her desired word count) and exactly when she will carve out the time to do it. The novelist leaves our session with the *intention* to spend 3 hours this Saturday morning writing the Mary and Frank scene (*action*).

At our next session, she may report that she did not write the scene intended but produced something else instead: that her idea evolved from Frank having an affair to Frank taking secret ballet lessons. Or she may have abandoned the character of Frank altogether and written her scene with two women and taken the novel in a completely different direction. This does not matter one jot so long as the novelist was engaged in the deep work that her story requires. Honest reflection will help her determine that.

If, on the other hand, the novelist wrote very little or did not write at all, this is also feedback with which we can work. Through the process of *reflection* we discover what got in her way. Was it something external such as urgent paid work or family commitments? Or was it an internal obstacle such as anxiety, or loss of faith in her project, or the fear of failure? Perhaps something happened during that week that caused her to lose confidence in her abilities as a writer—receiving a rejection, for example.

Reflection provides the information needed to reset the goal—see the example with Lisa that follows. The novelist again applies *intention, action, reflection* to the new goal set.

 For Home Use

The exercise is seemingly very simple but needs a little thought and effort to be truly effective. The key is in setting the goal, the *intention*. The acronym S.M.A.R.T. (Specific, Measurable, Achievable, Relevant, and Time-Bound) is useful here.

The novelist, for example, aimed to write a particular scene at a particular time and not merely to write: therefore, her goal was *specific*.

She aimed to write for a *measurable* number of hours or produce a set number of words.

It was *achievable* both in terms of scope and because its execution was within her control. You cannot set as a goal to sell your novel to a publisher because they may not wish to buy it, but you can commit to send it out to twenty agents or, indeed, self-publish.

The task was *relevant* in that the scene was part of the novel.

Finally, she aimed to complete the task by our next session. It was therefore *time-bound*.

If trying this at home, I suggest you use a journal to log the date, the task, and your reflections. If you apply yourself and don't give up, you *will* gain insights and make progress.

Client Results

Lisa is a PhD candidate struggling to make progress on her thesis. At the end of our first session, she sets herself the goal to produce 500 words a day, five days a week.

"Treat yourself as though you are in the laboratory," I tell her. "Simply note what happens. Think of your discoveries as findings, neither good nor bad."

"So, how did it go?" I ask Lisa at our next session.

She looks glum. "It was okay for the first few days," she says. "Then, as usual, I felt I needed to read another article and double-check books I'd already read . . ."

Lisa describes how she'd disappeared down a rabbit hole of research. She missed her daily word target, became despondent, and wrote nothing further.

We talk it through. Her need for further research is valid but unhelpful when producing words.

"It's the same with editing," I say. "Trying to write and edit at the same time is like driving with the brakes on."

Together, we set a new goal: to write 850 words a day, three days a week, with two days set aside for research. On a "writing" day, if Lisa feels the need for more information, she will type herself a prompt such as "research" or "clarify" and continue writing.

At the following session, Lisa reports that the new scheme is working well and that she achieved the weekly word count. "The anxious part that usually stops me writing when I feel unsure was soothed by knowing I'd be able to research later in the week," she says. "Amazingly, I kept going."

"That's great," I say encouragingly. But I know that the new scheme might not work indefinitely. "Intention, Action, Reflection means that you'll always have the feedback you need to adjust your goals as the work develops," I remind her. She nods her agreement.

 ## About Vinita Joseph

Vinita specializes in coaching academics and creatives. Her previous experience as a family lawyer and a long-standing mindfulness practice brings a potent combination of strategic thinking and spaciousness to her coaching practice.

Vinita became accredited as a coach when she was doing a PhD in Creative Writing and identified a gap in the support provided by her university. She now uses creativity coaching to help PhD students and academics complete their research projects. Her scheme won an award for teaching innovation in 2016. A writer herself, she also works with creatives.

Vinita Joseph—Coaching Solutions

https://vinitajoseph.com/

Don't Solve the Problem 11

Drew Richardson

Exercise Purpose

This exercise helps creatives get unstuck and keep moving forward with a project or a practice.

 Exercise Description

Creative people like to solve problems. It's a big part of what we do. This conundrum is often an opportunity to come up with a solution that's artistic, personal, fun, and unexpected. But some problems come along and derail us, and the creative train will not arrive until the problem is solved.

As a professional fool, I take inspiration from the classic clowns of film and stage, such as Buster Keaton and Charlie Chaplin. Got your foot stuck in a bucket? Don't spend all morning trying to get it off when you are late for work—keep the bucket on your foot and catch the bus and keep your job! In other words, don't solve the problem.

First, observe that a problem, big or small, is taking up a good part of your creative time. Define the problem for further clarity: ask yourself, what's the problem?

Take a few relaxing breaths and then, simply, don't solve the problem. Go on with the work, as foolish as that sometimes might be or look. Notice the thoughts that might come up, such as, "I can't continue because I don't know what I'm doing if I don't put this piece of the puzzle in place." Enjoy the absurdity of the situation.

You might find the problem gets solved while you go about your business and continue working. While climbing a ladder, the bucket stuck on your foot gets dislodged and falls off as you try to climb higher. Or maybe new discoveries happen because of the problem you left in place. That bucket on your foot might have kept you from stubbing your toe or is the thing that you need to kick a football harder and higher.

 In Session or as Homework

In practice, whether advising a student or coaching a performer, I would begin by asking the art-maker what he or she is working on. How they answer this question sets the possibilities. If they have a work-in-progress, I ask what problems are getting in the way or what the biggest problem is. Then we can tackle thinking about what it would be like not trying to solve it. If the performer isn't working on a piece at the moment, say because a show has just ended, then we can daydream about what it might be like to have a problem and not solve it.

Why does this process work? First, I have my client try to imagine what not solving the problem might look like. Just imagining the idea of not solving the problem can be enough to show the way forward. If that isn't enough, I would give them the assignment of going back to their work and spend some time creating without solving the problem. I frame this as "just a game," so they can have fun with this. The experiment might turn into a "complete disaster," but they can always return to their previous ways of working.

I check in to see how manageable this risk is for them. Do they need to set the goal of ignoring the problem for a week, a day, an hour, or just 15 minutes? Variations on this exercise might include creating a problem just to ignore it and, for the strong of heart, accumulating multiple problems without trying to solve any of them. Another tactic is to write the problem on a big piece of paper, to then attach it to the wall on the other side of the room, and to have the client's subconscious mind work on solving it while his or her conscious mind is actively "not solving it."

 ## For Home Use

An actor goes home to practice not solving the problem. The problem is serious trouble memorizing lines. "That's pretty easy not to solve," the actor thinks ironically. "I just don't memorize my lines, show up to the audition and do an amateurish job, and I don't get the part. That doesn't sound very smart!"

The actor sits down with the script and looks at all the notes and underlined words and realizes memorizing isn't the problem. The problem is that the actor has no sense of who this character is and can't keep learning the lines until he gets a better grasp. Now, that is a problem not to solve!

The actor works on the monologue without knowing who the character is or who the playwright imagined the character to be. The work feels awkward and uncomfortable, but the actor is up and working, playing, trying out different things, being present with the words and the situation.

Flashes of insight about the character appear and, after a few days, the actor realizes that the lines have been memorized. In addition, the actor discovers that this character's main quality is obliviousness. It's an understanding that makes a strong connection for the actor, who now feels confident showing it to others.

 ## Client Results

I needed to use this exercise myself in order to complete this section. I've used this exercise with students, advisees, and colleagues as a teacher, mentor, and director, and it's one of my top ten ways to think like a fool and aid creative problem-solving. But the search for memories, for stories, for examples was proving to be difficult and taking up a lot of time.

Then a voice in my head said, *don't solve the problem!* There it was. To finish writing this exercise, I had to stop searching for specific examples, I had to stop trying to remember, and I had to write. What to write about? About this! And here I am, solving the problem by not solving the problem.

This section came as a result of my own advice and freed me up from the limitations of having to find the right and best answer. I have my example, me, and I have my exercise written. And now my mind is flooded with images of ways of using this exercise in class and rehearsals. But I don't need those images right now, as I am done. How lovely and how foolish!

 About Drew Richardson

Drew Richardson is a professional fool who directs, teaches, coaches, and performs. He is best known as the first person in the 21st century to have new silent movies shown in major motion picture theaters around the U.S. Richardson's solo theatre shows have toured nationally and internationally, including the International Comedy Arts Festival in China. He also performed with Squonk Opera in a tour of their Broadway show, Bigsmorgasbordwunderwerk. His current area of writing and research is how foolish thinking can solve problems creatively. Most recently, he has been teaching acting and clowning in universities and colleges as a visiting professor of theatre.

Contact: www.DrewRichardson.net

Vanquish Your No's and Overcome Procrastination

12

Jude Walsh

Exercise Purpose

Many creatives struggle with procrastination, sometimes to the point where we never actually start our work, much less finish it. When we procrastinate, what we are really doing is telling ourselves no. Let's look at what saying no means with regard to creating with purpose and ease. I'll deconstruct some no's and offer a strategy or two to vanquish them.

 ## Exercise Description

Have you ever had a great idea and you immediately write down the heart of it, thinking, "Oh, I can't wait to flesh this out?" Then weeks later the idea is still nagging at you, but now the nag is layered with guilt about why you haven't done something with it? This is a fear of *beginning* and you saying no to starting.

Or, you have the most smashing idea for a novel and in a burst of energy you outline the plot, and over the next few days you write three or four kick-ass scenes and then . . . nothing. Suddenly, there are a million other things that you think need to be done and need to take priority, when actually you have hit a wall with the writing but don't want to admit it. This is fear of *completion* and you saying no to the joy of a finished work.

Or, have you ever read a call for submissions and thought, "That's perfect for me. It is exactly what I need to advance my practice right now"? The submission closing date was weeks out when you read the notice, but now it is three days before submissions close and you have not done one thing? Ouch. This is fear of *rejection* and you saying no so as to avoid the possibility that your work might not be considered good enough and rejected.

In each of these scenarios, you are procrastinating by telling yourself no and, as a result, not moving forward. By examining your self-imposed no a bit more closely, and ferreting out what the consequences and possible benefits of the no are, you can move past them and return to a productive mindset and practice.

In the first scenario, you are saying no before you start; if you never start, nothing can be produced. In the second, you are saying no to completion, denying yourself the satisfaction of a finished project. In the last, you are avoiding rejection. In all three of these cases, procrastination is sheltering you from putting your work into the world. Why would we say no to ourselves in this way?

Why would we not want our work in the world, making a difference? While all artists create from the heart and soul, our mind can wreak havoc on our ego. What will people think? What if I am not the artist or writer I think I am? What if my submission is rejected? What if my work is just ignored?

What does telling ourselves no do for us? What is the underlying value? If we never write, no one will ever read it and no one will ever find fault with it. It will remain this terrific idea, full of potential to tap at a later time. If we never finish the novel or the painting, it remains in the world of possible, just momentarily shelved. All these no's protect us from judgment and rejection; the benefit is that we are "safe."

If we follow the no all the way through, though, safe does not feel so good. We deny ourselves the potential pleasure of having our efforts warmly received. We deny ourselves feedback that may advance us as artists. We deny ourselves the satisfaction of bravely putting our work out there and knowing that we have done our best and that it is indeed enough.

⚙ In Session or as Homework

Use these questions to examine your procrastination and help unpack how saying no is helping you or hindering you:

1. What will happen if I don't complete this project? What will I lose? What will I gain?
2. What will happen if I do complete this project? What is the best outcome? What is the worst?
3. How can I switch from a no mindset to a yes mindset, thus getting my work into the world?

Let's use avoiding submission as an example.

1. If I do not get this in on time, I will have missed the opportunity to be considered. If I do not submit, then I do not have to face the fear of rejection and the anxiety of waiting for a response.
2. If I do submit, the obvious best outcome is acceptance and success. But then there is the shadow side of success, that the work will be seen and judged. Or perhaps the rejection will be so discouraging I might stop work altogether.
3. If I do not submit, then I am guaranteed a no. If I do get a rejection, that does not mean my work is not of value; it may just mean this is not the right place for it. If the rejection comes with a critique, I will have the opportunity to improve the work and submit again. Rejection is part of living a creative life. These thoughts help loosen the ego's grip on outcome and open the possibility of acceptance.

🏠 For Home Use

In addition to looking at how telling yourself no is stopping your productivity, try this: state the concern and then turn it around to a positive affirmation.

For example: "This journal has a ridiculously low acceptance rate. My writing will not make the cut, so why bother?" Turn that around to: "I am a good writer and I believe in my work. I am saying yes to this opportunity, and I embrace whatever the outcome is. I will either rejoice and be delighted or I will learn from the experience and get accepted next time. Either way I am moving my work forward."

Taking time to examine how saying no to your own work helps or hinders you and then creating an affirmation to bolster your courage will help loosen the grip of procrastination.

 ## Client Results

I use this practice in coaching sessions with my clients. I find this most successful with clients who have a long list of "Yes, but . . ." responses to any suggestions I make. "Yes, but . . ." is simply a "no" in disguise. We work together, using the questions to unpack what that no is really doing.

After working through the process a few times together, it becomes a coaching shortcut. I can say. "Have you asked yourself the three questions?" If not, we do them together. But eventually they become a self-help strategy. Sometimes, once they understand the three questions, they can jump straight to stating the concern and turning it into a positive affirmation. Either way, clients move forward with their work.

While procrastinating about writing this piece, I reminded myself that this practice has been enormously successful with my clients, and part of my commitment to creative citizenship is to share what works. By saying no to writing it, I was limiting the number of folks who could learn the practice and move forward. My positive affirmation was: "This strategy has helped many writers, so stop procrastinating and get words onto the page. Putting the information into print will make the information more widely available." And so, procrastination conquered.

**

 ## About Jude Walsh

Jude Walsh is a creativity and mindset coach. She is the author of *Post-Divorce Bliss: Ending Us and Finding Me* (Morgan James, 2019) and writes self-help, memoir, and fiction. She teaches classes on writing the personal essay, developing a creative practice, and mindset. Jude loves working with women post-divorce and all creatives ready to pivot to something new. Her superpower is that she can see the best in you, see talents you may not know you have, and help you see it too. You can connect with her at www.secondbloom-coaching.com.

Create Your Essence List 13

April Bosshard

Exercise Purpose

This exercise allows creatives to connect with what matters most to them at a meta level. An awareness of one's unique set of personal values, captured in an Essence List, serves as a powerful compass for accessing inspiration, motivation, and even healing.

 Exercise Description

This two-step exercise requires a blank sheet of paper, a pen or pencil, and about 15 minutes of quiet time.

Step 1. Draw a line down the middle of the page to make two columns. In the first column, list the eight things you want most out of life—*more than anything else*. These are the big things, often expressed in a single word, such as Connection, Love, Peace, Beauty, Success, Pleasure, Truth, Justice, etc. Write quickly and intuitively. There are no right answers, only *your* answers.

When you're done, have a look over your words. If you wrote several words, or a specific thing, such as, "Write a great novel," try to reduce that to the essence of what that means *to you*. Is it "creative expression" or "creative success"? Or simply "creativity" or "success"? You're looking for the meta meaning here. If you wrote, "Have enough money for the rest of my life," does that reduce down to a word like "security" or a word like "abundance"? Play with the words a little bit, but not too much. First thought, best thought works well for this exercise. At the same time, you want to reach for the underlying essence, the deeper meaning of those things, so that you end up with a list of eight single words or short phrases.

Step 2. In the second column, across from your original list, write down that word's opposite. Not its exact language opposite, but *an opposite that rings true for you*. Again, write quickly and intuitively. The words on your first list have a "resonance" for you; their meanings are deep and wide and not necessarily easy to explain. If you wrote down "love," what you mean by love may not be the same as someone else's meaning, and so your opposites may be different. Your opposite to love might indeed be hate, but it also might be loss, indifference, alienation, or loneliness. Again, there is no *right* answer, just *your* answer.

After creating this two-columned list, keep it somewhere safe. You might want to transfer the words to a recipe card and pin it to your wall or tuck it in your purse or wallet. This Essence List becomes a personal reference tool both for your life and your creative processes.

 In Session or as Homework

If a client is having a hard time sticking to a project, or accessing enough energy to finish it, seeing their work through the lens of the Essence List can be reinvigorating and motivating. Once the list is created, a coach can ask, "Which words on the list are showing up in the project?" Someone feeling stuck or blocked can be asked to locate the word on their Essence List that connects to their *original inspiration* for that stalled project.

Things get interesting when you start exploring the opposites. If, for example, the original inspiration for a project was rooted in joy, the client can be encouraged to look at the opposite of joy on their list. Is that opposing energy trying to sabotage the work? If their opposite is sadness, or perhaps despair or misery, a coach can ask if the client is experiencing sadness, misery, or despair around the project. Maybe they're sad that it's not all they hoped it would be, or they're despairing at never truly "making it" as an artist, or because one aspect of creation feels miserable to them, that one element is now overshadowing the whole process. You can then help them get back in touch with the positive value on the list.

Many writers struggle to create enough authentic conflict and motivation for their characters, and they can be encouraged to create an Essence List for one or more of their characters. It can be a powerful resource for character development and a compass for identifying relevant conflicts. Since good stories pit strong values against each other, writers who are courageous enough to make the most of opposing values end up accessing a lot of dynamic story energy.

For Home Use

The Essence List can be returned to many times and for a variety of situations.

For inspiration when creating a new project, we can ask ourselves: Which value is driving this project? Or: Which one or more values do I intend to explore with this project?

It can be a source of motivation if we're struggling to maintain momentum. We can ask: Which value have I fallen out of touch with to get this work done? We can look to the list of opposites to see which forces may unconsciously be working against us.

During stressful or depressing times, this list can be a source of healing if we interpret it as "what I need right now." At low points, we often need something on that list (peace, truth, connection, or a feeling of success or power) because those are the things that matter most to us. We can then find a way to experience something that represents a sense of peace, truth, or connection *to us*. We can also peruse the opposites list and identify where our difficult feelings are coming from (a sense of powerlessness, isolation, loneliness, inner chaos, etc.).

Stepping back and examining our struggles and successes from this meta level gives us a unique perspective on our creative process and our individual life, because what we care about most lies at the heart of *what* we create and *how* we create.

 ## Client Results

In workshops with writers, I'm always impressed by how focused people are while coming up with their lists, though sometimes they need a bit of encouragement to be loose, intuitive, and less literal.

In one workshop, Sandra's first list included the sentence, "I want everyone in my family to be happy." Asked to investigate the idea a little more, she was able to simplify the idea to "relationship harmony" and then eventually to the single word "harmony." She realized how important harmony was to her in her personal life as well as her creative process. (And she was surprised to discover that her main character felt the same way!)

Sandra also had the word *love* on her list, which didn't surprise her, but what did were the words she chose for love's opposite. They included neglect, indifference, and being ignored. These words uncovered some life issues related to her career coming to an end and her children growing up and moving away.

Alan, a middle-aged man in another workshop, was insistent when he wrote, "Write a bestseller and have it turned into a movie." I asked him to consider what he wanted out of that. Was it success, recognition, or esteem? Or maybe he wanted to be impactful, powerful, or make connections with a large number of people. In the end, he simplified his words to "respect." On the way, he had a profound insight about an old need to impress his father by doing something important. It turned out that a need for respect drove some of his main character's motivation as well.

Invariably, people in a group share one or more values on their Essence List, but the particular combination of the eight is always unique, as are the personal meanings underlying the words (especially when factoring in the opposites). There are always enough variations to reveal that each person is unique, but there are also enough similarities to reveal that many values are shared collectively.

What we want most in life is rooted in the values we hold most deeply. This is true for everyone. When creatives can identify the values that matter most to them, and choose to create work grounded in values-based themes, not only do they stay connected to personal meaning in their process and projects, but they also have a greater chance of tapping into what is personally meaningful to the audiences they wish to reach.

 ## About April Bosshard

April Bosshard is a writer, painter, story coach, and workshop facilitator who works with clients around the world. Her keen awareness of story principles and deep understanding of the writer's craft and the creative process allow her to help writers face many of the complex issues that arise when creating stories and sticking to the writing process. Find out more at www.deepstorydesign.com.

Making a Space

14

Clare Thorbes

Exercise Purpose

Making a Space is a combined cognitive and visualization exercise that helps creatives delay and change their habitual responses to negative comments about their work.

When you're faced with anger or barbed comments about your creative work, it can feel like the words are invading your body and bowling you over. The first instinct is to lash out, fall apart, or run away. These are normal responses to perceived threats. You put everything you have into your creative work, so negative comments feel like a personal attack. They may even tempt you to give up your passion!

If you deliberately make a space between the trigger and your response, you can give yourself time to think about and choose how you will respond to the trigger.

 Exercise Description

To begin the exercise, remind yourself that you're solidly planted right where you are and that you're completely safe. Take several slow, deep, calming breaths.

Take notes. This will distract your body from automatically tensing up, and it will also give you a record that you can later compare with your initial perceptions. You might be surprised at the disparity between the two, as emotional arousal can distort what you hear.

Imagine that you're creating a space between the other person's words (the trigger) and your reaction. The space could be a lake, a canyon, or even the room you're in.

Visualize the space slowly widening, increasing the separation between you and the trigger. You can still hear the words, but it's as if the person is floating farther away. You're at an increasingly safe remove, so the comments can't penetrate as readily. Imagine that the person's words are arrows plopping harmlessly into the growing chasm between you.

When the encounter is over, you may feel some lingering physical tension or a residual emotional sting. Decompress by releasing, analyzing, and celebrating. Dance up a storm, yell and stamp your feet, punch the air, or let out a primal scream.

Now look over your notes. Is there something you need to change in your work? Were the comments completely off the mark, or did they contain grains of truth that you need to pay attention to?

Finally, congratulate yourself! By not firing back a retort in the moment, you avoided alienating someone who might be important to your career at some point or who could become a friend you can count on to tell you the truth.

Making a Space works best if you practice it regularly, either by imagining someone's hurtful words, role-playing with a friend, or using the exercise when you encounter milder triggers. Then, when you face severe provocation, including someone deliberately trying to undermine you, you'll be more likely to remember that you don't *have* to react right away, nor do you have to react with anger or distress.

 In Session or as Homework

In a creativity coaching session, I ask a client to recall or imagine a situation in which she felt wounded by someone's comments about her work. We go through the Making a Space exercise step by step. I provide the client with encouragement, validation, and information at each step, and the client learns and experiences the empowerment of *choosing* her response to a situation.

Making a Space can also be a client's homework between sessions. If a client and I decide that this would be the best approach, we take some time to explore any uncertainty or resistance she may feel towards the exercise. It helps to remind the client that in all areas of life, habitual responses can be quite ingrained and difficult to shift, but that with time and practice, as well as a coach's support, the shift can occur.

At the next session, I check in with the client and discuss any issues that came up, including the possibility that the client did not feel up to tackling the exercise. In that case, the client and I look at whether any underlying issues were feeding her resistance, and then we walk through the exercise together.

 For Home Use

Clients can employ this technique in other emotionally charged situations: the opening night of an art exhibition, when pitching a story idea, or when trying to resolve differences with bandmates. Again, it's best to practice the exercise first by creating a scenario that closely mimics the problematic situation, so that you can hone your skills in safe, progressive stages. You can gradually up the ante by having a friend role-play with you, and then re-create a difficult scenario with a small, supportive group. Even with the safest of scenarios, though, make sure you take the time to decompress as described earlier.

Client Results

One client used this exercise in a writer's group, in which she interpreted someone's feedback as generally hostile and cutting. The client was reluctant to share excerpts from her works-in-progress for fear of this person's reaction. On one occasion, the other person, after hearing one of the group pitch a story idea, said, "Oh, that'll never work!"

By picturing the critic moving away from her and by then later reading her notes, the client was able to see that the person's comments were blunt but not intended to be insulting, and were offered in the spirit of helping everyone to improve their writing.

Another client wanted to negotiate new hours for her day job to give her time to paint in the mornings. Her boss tended to be short-tempered and quick to dismiss any unconventional idea. Practicing Making a Space switched her focus from anticipating a nerve-wracking encounter that would end with her in tears to devising strong arguments in support of her new schedule.

During the meeting, she visualized a widening space between her and her boss, and discovered that she wasn't as startled by his loud voice and vehement gestures. She was able to see past his angry demeanor and address his real concerns. She convinced him to do a three-week trial of her new schedule. In the end, her boss had to admit that she was more focused and productive, and he authorized an indefinite extension of the new schedule. The client got the precious morning painting hours she needed, and her boss gained an employee who was fully committed and present during her office hours.

The practice of Making a Space can include nurturing a vision of yourself as an unflappable, open-minded person who maintains positive relationships with the important people in your creative life—and the rest of your life. Over time, you may find that you become less immediately reactive in general.

** **

 ## About Clare Thorbes

Clare Thorbes is a certified creativity coach based in Ottawa, Canada, who works with writers, visual artists, and performers. She believes that all those who are called to create deserve a chance at a fulfilling life in the arts, and her goal is to be her clients' ally as they build that life. Clare publishes *Block-Buster*, a creativity newsletter, on her website: www.clarethorbescreativitycoach.com. She is also a visual artist (www.clare thorbes.com; www.facebook.com/clarethorbesportraits), and a multilingual translator and editor who has helped novelists and nonfiction writers across Canada bring their creations to life. Contact Clare via her website: www.clarethorbescreativitycoach.com, or by email: clare.thorbes@gmail.com.

Problem-Solving Against the Clock

15

Kassie Cowles

Exercise Purpose

This exercise uses *play* as a strategy to help blocked creatives push through problems or questions they are having trouble resolving in their work. It encourages creatives to get out of the mindset of work and into the mindset of play to reveal possible solutions and opportunities to developing work and solving creative problems.

 Exercise Description

If you've ever played Pictionary or Charades, then you'll understand the premise of this exercise. You will need a big piece of paper or a whiteboard and marker with a large tip so that what you produce is big enough to see from a distance. It's important in this exercise to work big—the bigger the better, in fact—so that you physically work outside the smaller confines of a computer screen and break out of any fixed ideas and habits in the mind and body.

Thinking too much or too deeply about a creative problem can often make the problem seem bigger than it is. One way to dislodge all possibilities in a practical way is to work with and against time (and a healthy bit of adrenalin) to reveal solutions to the creative problems you're facing. This exercise is also a great way to generate solutions to creative problems without the usual biases and barriers we often have when we are sitting in front of our computer screens trying to come up with solutions.

Creative problems can include not knowing what to do next in work, not knowing how to get your characters out of a predicament, not knowing how to further the plot, or not knowing how you really feel about what you're writing or creating. Sometimes we can be afraid of shifting the framework or focus of our projects too much because it may mean a lot more work, but if it means creating a truer, more honest, or more exciting piece of work, then it's worth the exploration.

In Session or as Homework

This exercise or problem-solving game is simple:

1. Write your problem, challenge, or question in the middle of a big piece of paper or on the whiteboard.
2. Set a timer for 3 minutes. An old-fashioned egg timer is best, as the ticking of the seconds adds to the pressure and drama in a productive way.
3. Once the time starts, frantically write every conceivable word, phrase, or idea that comes to mind in relation to the problem you are trying to solve. Don't hold back or edit. Don't waste time on complete sentences; don't second-guess yourself; and don't worry if the words or images that are coming to you are relevant or not. Just write vigorously and capture everything that comes to you, without stopping for 3 minutes.
4. When the timer goes off and your 3 minutes are up, take a few steps back and look at what you have written. Is there anything that surprises you? Are there ideas that intrigue you? Are there words, images, or phrases that seem related somehow to one another? Do you recognize any patterns that could suggest an underlying solution or path of inquiry?
5. Circle the top three to five words, images, or phrases that seem the most exciting, confusing, or promising. Then, write one of the words or phrases on the whiteboard or on another large piece of paper and do the exercise again, setting the timer for 3 minutes and writing any associations, ideas, images, or phrases that come to you in relation to the word, while keeping your project in mind.
6. Do this as many times as you need to generate ideas and associations that may not have come to you in conventional ways.
7. Once you've done this exercise as many times as you need, start making connections between what has arisen for you. Draw bold lines connecting ideas and images. Circle, annotate, scribble: make a mess! The point of this exercise is to loosen your grip on how you conventionally problem-solve and create and allow for new connections and possibilities. Again, work big. Use a whole wall if you need to, so that the process is both physical as well as mental.

An alternative way of doing this exercise is to work in a team or in collaboration with one or more people. For example, you could explain to a trusted collaborator what your problem, challenge, or question is. Have your collaborator do this exercise in exactly the same way on your behalf in front of you, against the clock.

See what she comes up with when the stakes (for her) are low and she can generate any idea she wants. Not only can this be quite funny and outrageous (and remind you not to take it all too seriously), but it can be transformative to have an outside perspective on possible solutions and directions to a challenge you are facing.

 For Home Use

This exercise is easily adapted for home use by following the instructions and modifying them as necessary.

Client Results

I have assigned this exercise for homework to clients with great results and have also done it together during one-on-one sessions. Clients find the aspect of *play* helps them access ideas and approaches that they would not have otherwise considered.

Having the large pieces of paper to look at together is also incredibly helpful for making connections and developing possible leads. The paper or whiteboard can then be displayed in the client's studio or personal workspace as a stimulus as the work develops, and as a reminder that this exercise can always be done again when necessary.

This activity also works very well for collaborative projects. *Time* is a great collaborator, and the act of creating a container of time within which something must be immediately produced is very effective and freeing. I have done it many times with my theatre students when they are devising an original piece of work and need to generate ideas and approaches to creating. It's a great way to begin a project from scratch, and it can work to free ideas and solutions when the group is facing problems they are having a difficult time solving.

**

 About Kassie Cowles

Kassie Cowles has worked in arts education for thirteen years. She is a theatre and literature teacher, writer, and creativity coach, working in communities around the world. She is particularly inspired by the process of collaboration and in ushering new work into existence. She can be reached directly at kassi.cowles@gmail.com.

Relaxed, Determined, Forward

16

Nefeli Soteriou

Exercise Purpose

Relaxed, Determined, Forward is designed to empower clients to successfully undertake the task of revisiting their material. Although tailored for the screenwriter, a coach can modify it for a variety of artistic mediums.

 Exercise Description

The coach guides the client to complete the exercise in ninety days and coordinates the time frame of the follow-up sessions in between.

Designed with a focus on mindfulness, Relaxed, Determined, Forward reminds the client of the significance of self-care, how to calm down while in physical discomfort, how to ignore limiting thoughts, and how to take their creative work to the next step. The coach shares the following introduction with the client:

Imagine your creative zone as a red cotton string dangling below your navel. As life progresses, knots may be formed, resulting in an uncomfortable tightening around your waist. One knot is perhaps that you are physically exhausted; maybe your day job is demanding, as are your other responsibilities at home. You jot ideas down on your smartphone and you take writing classes to improve, but you can't find the time to realize a further edit.

In the following weeks, you may think that what you wrote is too old and that it would be better if you drafted something new. You start to write again, which means that you haven't effectively used what you've already written. As the months go by, another knot is added, this one of disappointment. Then your writer friend calls to share that her book is being published and there you are, not being able to decide which scenes to arrange for a cold reading with actors. More knots!

1. Relaxed

For the most part, things don't simply happen in life. We create them. We manage life stressors best when we tenderly care for our body and select a home environment that's just right for us to nurture our well-being. Regardless of your age, know that it is possible to manage day-to-day work and responsibilities at home with more ease, as you nourish yourself with foods that are easy to digest, non-processed, and mainly plant-based. Drink clean water; leave electronics out of the bedroom. Walk in your neighborhood 20 minutes three to five times a week, or find one recreational activity you really love and stick to it.

Love your brain and feed it healthy fats like avocados and omega 3's, treat it with dark chocolate, work it with new learning and coordination activities, and limit your alcohol intake and other chemical substances, for example, synthetic pills. Start every day with intention, gratitude, and appreciation.

What might help you unwind after work? Is it a mutual agreement with a partner not to talk for the first 30 minutes after you reach home? To quickly shower to rid yourself of work smells? To change into comfortable clothes? To write an appreciation card? You might mark down the three major benefits that your day job brings you, for example, "it pays the bills," "retirement savings," and "allows vacation time." Keep the card in your wallet, and when you have a frustrating workday, pull it out and read it aloud.

Who constitutes your support system? Prioritize your time so that you mingle with caring individuals who have respect for self and for others. The main idea is to convince yourself that you can lead a more relaxed life and then to actually live it.

2. Determined

What does determined look like? Creating fills your heart with joy and lights you up! You spend at least 20 minutes daily creating. You utilize lunch breaks to write, during a hands-free commute, or with your morning tea. You have an open mind to continue pushing through and even increase your creative work time in the near future.

Truth be told, some days are better than others. Should you break your commitment to yourself, work on refraining from judgment and simply start again the next day! Sticking to this habit makes all the difference in the long haul. The main idea is to realize that you can be relaxed and determined at the same time. It's not one or the other!

3. Forward

List everything you wrote and have not revisited yet, from screenplay scenes, to short or long stories, dialogue snippets, or screenplay characters you developed. Highlight one or two that you aim to revise. Then proceed and open the first document.

During this time, you may face real distractions. Sign out from your email accounts, your chat apps, and from social media and web browsers. Turn off the phone, of course turn off the TV, and put on your favorite music if it helps you write. Lean back. Bring awareness to the moment and observe your breathing, taking deep breaths in from your nose and slowly exhale out from your mouth.

You may also encounter harsh, discouraging thoughts over the course of the ninety days. They can even make you question whether your own material is worth being seen by anyone. Know that thoughts are nothing but thin air. With that clarity in mind, you can return to your writing. You may also want to complete the following mini-exercise when these hindering patterns interfere:

1. Is the thought I just observed really true?
2. What do I really want to feel right now?
3. What am I willing to do to complete my writing task?

As you become more relaxed and more present, and also determined, writing and revising turn into a manageable routine.

Should you encounter other physical discomfort such as sweating palms or an increase in your heart rate, there is no need to feel disheartened. Continue working on naturally calming yourself down with deep breathing inhalations and exhalations. Repetition is your ally. Complete your breathing exercises and try again the next day. Consider setting a timer for starting and ending your creative work. Also, refrain from getting up from your chair until the timer is up.

By taking determined action and refining your steps each time you encounter challenges, and by also staying relaxed, you will succeed. "Relaxed, determined, forward" is your new mantra. You untangle your creativity knots one at a time, as you mindfully nurture your needs. Likewise, you change your state of mind by acknowledging your thoughts. In due time you will reap wonderful results from your efforts.

 ## In Session or as Homework

Clients are advised to keep a daily activity log and to report on their progress in follow-up sessions. These follow-up reports can become the subject and substance of subsequent sessions, as clients are helped to strategize ways to become more relaxed and more determined and to move forward.

 ## For Home Use

The exercise is designed for a workspace at home and can also be adapted for studio use. The main task is for clients to keep the two ideas of relaxation and determination in mind and to do those things that actually serve to relax them and help them maintain focus and determination. By using the mantra "relaxed, determined, forward" and keeping track of their efforts for ninety days, they will make real progress in creating new work or revising old work.

 ## Client Results

Relaxed, Determined, Forward has proven valuable to clients of mine who needed to accelerate their productivity and take their work from where it was to the next level. Clients who were unable initially to review their screenplays learned to focus and successfully revise and complete them.

**

About Nefeli Soteriou

Nefeli Soteriou loves nature, exercise, and self-expression through art, adores animals, is interested in integrative medicine, produces indie narrative films and photography projects, holds an M.F.A. in Film and Media Arts, and is a Creativity Coach, an NYS Holistic Counselor, and an Energy Healer. If you'd like to learn more about Nefeli's work as a coach, please visit www.nefelisoteriou.com.

The Confidence Shop Visualization

17

Angela Terris

Exercise Purpose

If you could buy yourself a bit of confidence, what would that look like? Here's a quick exercise helping creatives visualize that one specific thing, confidence, that can make a real difference in their creative growth. Included are seven thought-provoking questions to deepen the experience and help bring greater clarity and positive progress.

 Exercise Description

This visualization is simple to use. All you need to do is find a quiet space where you won't be disturbed for a few minutes and close your eyes.

Now, imagine yourself standing outside a building called "The Confidence Shop." As you look at it, you feel intrigued and want to go inside. As you enter, you become aware of a room filled with curiosities.

After a few moments, a shop assistant comes forward and asks you if they can be of help. You say, "I would like to buy some confidence, please." The sales assistant wanders off, and you wait patiently to see what they'll bring.

As you wait, try to remain in a neutral state, with no preconceived ideas of what it "should" be that the sales assistant brings, and instead let your intuition guide you.

The sale assistant returns and hands you something. Look at it for a moment and wait to see what happens. If an image isn't revealing itself to you, look around the shop instead and see what catches your eye.

When you are satisfied that something has been revealed, open your eyes and come back into the room. Quickly capture your insights by jotting down a word or sentence describing what you saw.

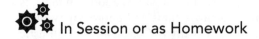 In Session or as Homework

You can use the following questions to expand on your findings:

1. What is your intuition telling you that you may need in order to build confidence?
2. What difference would this make to you and your creativity if you had more of this?
3. Where do you hope this will lead?
4. Where might this already be happening, even just a little bit in your life, and how could it be amplified?
5. What do you need to know, do, or have in order to gain self-mastery and in order for this to happen?
6. Can you do this by yourself or do you need some support to guide you?
7. What one action can you take today to get the ball rolling?

Taking your answers into consideration, you now have specific details of what confidence means to you and what you hope it will bring. Your answers will highlight the areas of your creative practice that you can improve on and how to make that happen. Maybe you need to search for information, schedule time out, book a course, improve communication skills, or practice new techniques? Once pinpointed, the confidence you want is no longer a vague thing but something more substantial that you can learn and take action on.

 For Home Use

This exercise works beautifully at home and is easily adapted for home use, either for coach or creative, by making any necessary personalized changes to the instructions.

 Client Results

I use this exercise regularly with my coaching clients, since they often say that if they only had more confidence, they could do this or that. When pressed, clients are typically unsure of what they mean. This visualization is a good starting point to open up a discussion about this topic. It is easy to use, and I always ask permission of the client to make sure that he or she wants to proceed. I usually do this directly during the coaching call, and it is very easy to do that way.

As something for the client to do as homework, I ask them to identify how they will make their vision come true by writing a list of what they need to do, know, or have in order to achieve their goal and acquire more confidence. Next, I have them choose three tasks from their "how" list and commit to doing them. In our next call, we discuss what difference that has made for them, we identify any potential obstacles getting in their way, and we notice and celebrate how much braver they may now be feeling.

Sometimes a client will say that they don't visualize very well. I tell them that's okay and that maybe a word or a feeling will be revealed instead. I assure them that they can't "fail" at this and ask them to just keep an open mind.

You can change the shop description to any type of shop you wish, for example, The Motivation Shop, The Creative Success Shop, or The Inspiration Shop. Be playful and let your imagination roam free.

You can also record yourself speaking aloud The Confidence Shop visualization on your phone, and then you can play it back whenever needed. As you speak, leave mini-pauses between sentences to allow space for the imagery to emerge as you listen to the recording. When you're finished, reflect on the seven questions, create your personal "how" list, and start to make them happen.

To expand on this exercise, you could visualize yourself acting as if you were doing those tasks from your "how" list, all those little things that you have identified that would contribute towards building your confidence. You could also create an action board displaying images representing those actions needed to fulfill your confidence goal. If you look at your action board frequently, you are more likely to accomplish your actions. Keep refreshing your action board by removing images associated with tasks that have been completed and adding new action-images as you progress.

I used this exercise with a client who felt stuck in a rut with her creative business as a jewelry designer. Her business was moving forward well enough, but she had become lost in the everyday routine of making and fulfilling orders, resulting in a lack of enthusiasm and uncertainty about her direction.

The client mentioned that she felt a lack of confidence to implement the changes she knew that she needed to make. I introduced the idea of The Confidence Shop visualization to her as something that might help. What she imagined was a pair of sculptural earrings she had previously given to her sister as a present. With further questioning, it became apparent to her that she desired more time to experiment, be playful, work with new materials, and create one-off pieces, so that she could take her work to new and exciting places.

The actions she decided on were to schedule time solely for playful creation, to enroll in a course to improve her making skills, and to pencil in regular artist dates where she would sketch in nature, gaining fresh inspiration. All of these things helped boost her confidence in creating new work that excited her and helped create the space for the new work to emerge.

The client confirmed the success of the visualization by telling me, "You gave me time and space to explore how to increase my confidence and to imagine where I wanted to go next. The questions you asked helped me brainstorm possibilities and envision what I really want."

 About Angela Terris

Angela Terris is an artist, book author/illustrator, and creativity coach with a background in creative business, non-profit art organizations, and psychology. She now draws on her experience and knowledge to coach creatives to be bolder and braver in their artistic choices. She works mainly with individuals and creative businesses to develop calm, clear confidence in fulfilling their creative potential. Angela trained at Chelsea School of Art in London and set up her first creative business at the age of 22. She is best known for her book illustration, uplifting paintings, and passion for supporting creatives.

Website: www.angelaterris.com
Instagram: @angelaterris

Peace Treaty

18

A Dialogue Between the Critical Voice and the Creative Voice

Beatriz Martínez Barrio

Exercise Purpose

To soften the power of the critical voice and to allow creative energy to express its needs and desires.

 Exercise Description

When there is a creative blockage, there is usually an internal fight between a part of ourselves that wants to create (our creative force or inner child) and a part of us that prevents us from doing so (our critical voice or self-saboteur). In this exercise, clients are guided to connect with these two forces, name them, draw them, and make them engage in dialogue. The aim is to create a peace treaty that ends the internal fight and encourages small, creative actions.

Materials required: Crayons (or any other drawing material), pen, and paper.

Step 1. Make a list of the messages that your critical voice tells you. Try to be as exhaustive as possible and include all the critical beliefs that you tell yourself regarding your creative work and your self-image as an artist, e.g., "You don't have real talent," "Your work is boring," "You are too old to succeed," etc.

Step 2. Make a caricature drawing of your critical voice and name it. Try to picture the energy of this character and how it talks. Is it a dictator, a cynic, a tyrant, a sneak, a Machiavellian character? What color or colors do you associate with it? The drawing can be just an abstract shape that depicts the energy or any type of character drawing (male, female, animal, cartoon, fantasy). No drawing skills are required; a doodle or a childlike drawing are both welcome. Have fun doing it! Once you have finished, find a name for the character and write it on the drawing.

Step 3. Connect with your creative force and draw it. Try to picture a time when you felt totally immersed in a creative project. How did it feel? Find some adjectives that describe this energy. What color or colors do you associate with it? What shape? Make a drawing following the same instructions from step 2, name the character, and write it on the drawing.

Step 4. Incarnate the energy of your creative force by using your non-dominant hand to answer back, one by one, the messages on your list of "messages from your critical voice." The technique of using the non-dominant hand has been explored extensively by many therapists and has proven to be an excellent tool to connect with our subconscious, our interior voice, and our inner child. In this exercise, we are using it to represent our creative force.

Let yourself be surprised by what your non-dominant hand writes, almost as if it didn't belong to you. It usually has its own personality and a very direct way of expressing itself. For example, in answer to the belief of the inner critic, "You don't have real talent," a non-dominant hand might respond, "What is real talent? I do have talent. It is you who can't see it!"

Step 5. Place the two drawings next to your workspace. When your inner critic gets activated, think of it as a character and use the energy and the list of answers from the creative force to counteract its messages.

In Session or as Homework

The exercise can be used in a one-on-one session or in a group session.

Things to be considered: sometimes writing with the non-dominant hand can create feelings of stress and frustration since it puts us in contact with our own clumsiness. It can bring up memories from childhood lessons and make subconscious content emerge. It is important to advise clients that there is not a "right way" to write with the non-dominant hand and that any sorts of letters are welcome, even if they are illegible. Each person should find their own rhythm and take breaks in between if needed.

Warm-up Exercises

Warm-up exercises are recommended, especially if it is a person's first time writing with their non-dominant hand.

Gentle massage: First the right hand massages the left hand and then the left hand massages the right hand, in an effort to bring awareness of the differences between both hands.

Doodling: Alternate drawing doodles with one hand and then the other.

Symmetrical drawing: With a pen in each hand, try to make a symmetrical drawing using both hands at the same time.

Writing your name: Write your name five times using your non-dominant hand.

 For Home Use

An interesting variation of this exercise is to hold a dialogue between both hands. Any of the characters can start the dialogue. Once you've written a sentence with one hand, switch the pen to the other hand (you can also use a different color or different pen for each hand) and allow yourself a couple of seconds to connect with the energy of the other hand before answering. The dialogue can start as simply as "Hello, how are you today?" or it can be related to a creative block, a feeling, a thought, etc., for instance, "I'm feeling insecure about my new paintings. Why?"

 Client Results

The process of making a caricature of the inner critic is usually quite liberating. It helps to create some distance from the character, to not take it too seriously, and to approach it with a sense of humor.

The dialogue between two hands can be enlightening. Here is a short example of a dialogue from a client session:

R.H. (Right Hand): Hello, how are you?
L.H. (Left Hand): Weird. I feel clumsy. I want to write faster and nicer but I can't.
R.H.: Does it bother you that I write faster and better than you?
L.H.: Yes!!! It does. It bothers me to be compared to you all the time.
R.H.: I do it to help you grow.
L.H.: Well, it doesn't help. It makes me angry.
R.H.: Oh! I didn't know that. Sorry! How can I help?
L.H.: Stop putting pressure on me and accept that I have a different rhythm. It is okay to be slow!!!!

After this dialogue, the client realized there was nothing wrong with his own rhythm of creation, which was maybe "slower" than the demands of his inner critic. He made a drawing of his left hand and placed it next to his workspace. Every time he looked at it, it reminded him that it was okay to work more slowly.

 About Beatriz Martínez Barrio

Beatriz Martínez Barrio is a visual artist and art therapist based in Madrid, Spain. She uses art as an introspective and healing tool to help people reconnect with their own source of creativity and wisdom. She specializes in creative processes that involve the use of photography and video. For more than a decade, she has been coordinating the Master of Photography course at EFTI School of Photography in Madrid, where she helps students find their strengths in the visual languages. She also uses photography and art in her private art therapy sessions and creative workshops. She collaborates as a professor in various art therapy schools in Madrid. For more information, visit www.beatrizmbarrio.com.

Character Activation

19

Ariel Grace

Exercise Purpose

To help creatives step into new embodiments of self by using play-activated modeling of characters in their life.

 Exercise Description

Clients are led step-by-step through a process of defining a real or imaginary character and bringing it into their life in healthy ways.

Then, they are guided to reflect and integrate the learnings into their social or professional life as desired. This exercise can be both a playful and a profound way for clients to get reconnected with disowned or neglected aspects of themselves or to cultivate new ways they had not yet allowed themselves to consider.

Step 1: Character Ideation. Have your client jot down three characters from real life or imaginary ones that he admires. Then have him list the characteristics he likes, dislikes, feels envious of, or somehow feels "activated" by, noting what aspect or aspects particularly stand out.

Step 2: Character Charge. Have your client select the character that feels the most "charged" to use as a model for the exercise.

Step 3: Become the Character. Suggest that the client dedicate at least 15 minutes a day for five days to "being" this character. The client may want to use different clothing, real-world props, daydream or role-play, or speak differently.

It is important to bring this character out of the imaginal and into the sensory world through movement, voice, clothing, food, and other "real life" ways. How does the character dress? What does he say? Who does he associate with? What does he think about? How does he overcome challenges?

Step 4: Character Learnings. Suggest that your client pay particular attention to the aspect of this character that he felt a charge or "activation" around. How did it feel to spend time with that aspect? What were the thoughts and perceptions that the character had? Suggest that your client write down the feeling states that came up for him as he stepped into the character. For example, if this character is very carefree and the client feels very stifled, he might practice skipping and laughing to see what it feels like to be in another state of being.

✴ In Session or as Homework

In addition to this exercise, your client may want to try applying this concept to claiming (or reclaiming) identities (or titles) that they have struggled to adopt in their professional life.

Perhaps your client is already an artist, but they are struggling to feel confident in becoming an "author." This exercise can be used to help them embody an "author" and thus create new ideas and possibilities about how they would need to act to become an author.

Character Activation is a useful exercise for clients who feel overly serious, weighed down, or stuck in a particular role or way of being. It can be illuminating to step into new actions and habits that better support the role or way of being that a client longs to add to his life but has not given himself permission to test drive. This exercise presents a safe way to test out self-expression without feeling defined or threatened by it.

To get the most out of the exercise, it is necessary for a client to use his or her "right brain" and get into a curious or playful state. Suggest that your client create from the mind-set of a child and try the exercise while in a play state. In order to move into this state, he might want to spend time with children, watch a silly movie, or otherwise create a sense of nonsense and possibility. If the exercise is approached as "heavy homework," it will be much more difficult to immerse in the character, and thus the learning potential will be lessened.

Your client may find that he judges the character, the exercise itself, or his attempt to immerse completely in the play aspect, particularly if he is working with aspects of himself that feel heavy or serious. A potential solution to this is to exercise his body or get into a relaxed state prior to stepping into the character. A too-critical perspective will block the potential of the learnings.

Also, people often disown parts of their expression, and this can come out in unhealthy ways, if there is any shame or guilt around it. This exercise can be a way to express these difficult feelings more consciously while feeling supported and with a focus on learning. Likewise, this exercise can bring up feeling states such as sorrow, shame, guilt, anger, or resentment. This is often because the client's inner child has not felt tended to or listened to. It is important to create safety around this and support your client through any big emotions that may arise.

For Home Use

If you are adapting this for your own use at home, you can use your space and existing props in your home to support you. You might try incorporating music, food, and environmental and contextual cues that would fit this character, so as to deepen your experiential learning. Also, you may want to do this with other people who are willing to play additional characters.

Alternatively, you might leave your home and enter an environment that supports your character's personality. Using the author example, you might find that you are too distracted in your home but that you can picture your "favorite author" completing his manuscript with a cup of amazing coffee at a coffee shop. You can use this image to propel yourself to a coffee shop and "live" as that author. Notice what helps you to step into this role and what techniques suit your learning style.

 **Client Results**

When a client of mine tried this exercise, she was struggling with her self-confidence around singing in public. She found that by using a fictional character that had extra-human abilities to perform, she was able to change her attire slightly and create a particular style that supported her ability to easily step into the "singer" persona and feel confident in her voice when she stepped up on stage.

Another client of mine was struggling to become a workshop facilitator because of feeling stuck in a previous role as a teacher. While it seemed like a natural transition, it took considerable visualization and embodying the workshop facilitator character before she could actively step into the new role.

**

 About Ariel Grace

Ariel Grace is a coach for creatives, tech design consultant, intuitive, artist, and author. She enjoys co-creating new, collaborative ways to solve social challenges across different sectors. Connect with her online at https://linktr.ee/arielgracefull or on Instagram or Facebook at @ArielGraceFull.

Persona Mapping

20

Joran Slane Oppelt

Exercise Purpose

This exercise helps clients with identity, life purpose, and meaning issues and helps them increase their clarity, certainty, and confidence.

 Exercise Description

Supplies: Post-It® Easel Pad (or large sheets of paper), various colored Sharpies® (fine and chisel-tip), printed personality assessments

Persona Mapping is an individual exercise that can be used with creative and corporate clients. It allows the client to engage in a deep analysis of their personality and how they are perceived, as well as providing them with a full inventory of their strengths and sometimes latent or unrecognized capabilities.

The client reflects on language from multiple sources and perspectives before claiming a name, persona, or title that is fully their own and can be used in the workplace, on their business cards, or as a personal affirmation. The primary objective is to turn a cloud of words, culled from various assessments and peer observations, into a cohesive identity statement that is clear, precise, and empowering.

 In Session or as Homework

Step 1. Deploy at least three different personality assessments (DiSC, Meyers-Briggs, Fascination Index, 16 Personalities, StrengthsFinder, enneagram, etc.) to the individual or to the team in advance of the session.

Step 2. For group sessions, in addition to the assessments, you may also ask for the client's peers to describe their strengths and superpowers. This could be done in advance as a 360 interview (a specialized leadership tool) or on-site with team members in small groups. Gather the assessments and any other reporting (as PDFs or screen captures) in advance of the session, leaving yourself enough time to read and review.

Step 3. To begin the session, ask the client to go through all of their printed assessments and highlight or circle the words that stand out (i.e., protagonist, advocate, passion, power, stable, influence, cautious, engaging, learner, achiever, connoisseur, trust, effective coach, mesmerizes listeners, assertive when necessary, etc.).

Step 4. Using a Post-It® sheet or easel pad, ask the client to draw the bust or top half (head and shoulders) of a gingerbread-style human figure so that there is plenty of room to write both inside the figure as well as around the edges. This sheet should then be hung on the wall at eye level.

Step 5. Have the client write all of the highlighted language (and peer-provided description) outside the figure.

Step 6. Clients are encouraged to use different colors and different size text (including graffiti-style, bubble or block lettering, word art, etc.) when translating these words to the poster. They should have plenty of time to doodle, sketch, and choose which words are the most meaningful or relevant. Only positive or empowering language should make it to the poster.

Step 7. Having reviewed the assessments in advance (and based on what you know about the client), determine whether there are words, phrases, or key themes that are missing.

Step 8. When all the words have been mapped, the client is asked to stand back and reflect on the language and imagery outside the empty figure. They may stand a few feet from the wall, with eyes alternately open or closed, absorbing and feeling each word as if they're coming off the page.

Step 9. The client then begins to synthesize this language into one clear, concise (and fantastical) name or title they feel describes their highest and most powerful self. If they work in a corporate setting and are looking for a fancy new job title, we are looking for "Optimus Prime," not "Director of Operations." If they are a parent, we are looking for "Generous Life-Giver and Magic Moment Maker," not "Loving, Focused Full-Time Parent."

Step 10. Some coaching here may be necessary, but the words need to come from the client, not from you. You may prompt them by asking, "What's another fun word for . . . ?" Have them say the words out loud and ask them how it feels to claim them. Only words that make them feel alive, powerful, and in control should make it to the poster.

Step 11. Finally, the client writes this new persona or title (three to six words) big and bold inside the figure and decorates it with shapes, images, and more color. No language or words other than the new persona is to be used inside the figure.

Step 12. Before ending the session, I usually have the client turn their persona into an affirmation, facing the poster as if looking into a mirror and speaking aloud, "I am [their persona name here]." This may be an emotional moment as it is sometimes the first time the person is speaking or claiming this latent aspect or dimension of themselves out loud.

 ## For Home Use

This exercise can be used in large group settings, one-on-one-private coaching sessions, or as a self-directed exercise. In groups, there may be music playing and certain portions may be timed. If self-directed, a client may use a smaller sheet of paper (a large sketchbook or pages no smaller than 8.5" x 11") and take as long as a week to create the final image.

The final product should be colorful, bold, and vibrant. The final persona or title should be visible from across the room. This poster can then be hung in their office, bedroom, on their refrigerator, or near their altar at home.

 Client Results

I have used persona mapping successfully in all of the mentioned settings. During an all-staff, half-day retreat with a leading payments industry organization, more than fifty employees (using StrengthsFinder and peer-provided descriptions) claimed superhero-style names like "The Diva of Doing" and "The A-to-Zen Fixer."

In one half-day session, an executive team comprising a CEO, Director of Operations, and Creative Director (using DiSC, 16 Personalities, and Fascination Index) claimed the new titles "Prismatic Magic Maker," "Mystical Web Weaver of Nurturing Support," and "Compassionate Commander and Teacher of Teachers."

In a 90-minute, one-on-one coaching session, a client struggling to find purpose and clarity while juggling multiple personal and business roles (including intuitive, medium, teacher, mother, social media specialist, photographer, and more) arrived at the new title "Mystique Coach." She had never considered herself a coach before this session and has since launched her own creativity and intuitive arts coaching business.

Clients have said the following:

> "It's an eye-opener seeing all the words that describe me. It was interesting to see which words made me uncomfortable and which ones I connected with fully."
>
> "An empowering moment where you and your team get to see who you really are when you are working and living in your unique zone of genius."
>
> "I immediately felt more empowered to use my strengths to help the company grow and my team succeed. The persona mapping also allowed me to leverage and honor the strengths of my team."

 About Joran Slane Oppelt

Joran Slane Oppelt is an international speaker, author, creativity coach, facilitator, and consultant. He is the Creative Director at RIDG (Royal Innovation Design Group), owner of the Metta Center of St. Petersburg, and founder of Integral Church. Joran is the author of *Integral Church: A Handbook for New Spiritual Communities*; *Sentences*; *The Mountain and the Snow*; and co-author of *Order of the Sacred Earth* (with Rev. Dr. Matthew Fox) and *Transform Your Life: Expert Advice, Practical Tools and Personal Stories*. He is also an award-winning producer and singer-songwriter who has spoken around the world about spirituality and the innovation of religion. Reach him at joranslane@gmail.com; www.joranslane.com.

The Evening Review

Marj Penley

21

Exercise Purpose

This exercise is adapted from an exercise created by James and Susan Vargiu and appearing in the unpublished writings printed by The Psychosynthesis Institute when it was in Palo Alto, California.

In that exercise they write, "This exercise is best done as the last thing in the day. Just before going to sleep, review your day in your mind, playing it back like a movie, but backwards, beginning with where you are right now, and so on till the morning when you awakened. When you examine your day, do it as much as possible as a detached objective observer, calmly and clearly registering what has happened."

The purpose of the exercise is to gain insights into anything that might be hindering or helping one's creativity.

 Exercise Description

In the evening review, some of the points you might want to keep in mind are:

1. Were there any times during the day when you felt anxious or depressed?
2. While working as a creative, were there times when you were distracted?
3. Were there any times when you experienced procrastination or perfectionism?
4. Which different subpersonalities were predominant at different times during the day? (Subpersonalities are the many diverse psychological formations within our personality, such as the Child, the Lonely One, the Seeker, etc.)
5. What were the valuable qualities and what were the limitations related to each subpersonality? How did each help you or get in your way?

You will probably want to write down any insights you gain.

In Session or as Homework

The exercise is designed primarily to be done at night, with the results often discussed in session later with a competent coach or therapist. However, the exercise could be used as a guided fantasy during a session. In that case, the client would be assisted into a state of deep relaxation by the coach or therapist. After the client had reached such a deeply relaxed state, the client would be asked to focus on a particular creative concern or a particular subpersonality and then, using the Evening Review approach, would review the relevant experiences from the previous day. After the client has reviewed the previous day with the issue in mind and the guided fantasy has ended, the coach or therapist can discuss with the client any insights or understanding gained.

When the exercise is done at night just before going to sleep, the client would want to take notes related to the particular creative concern or particular subpersonality as he reviewed the day, noting each time that the particular creative concern or particular subpersonality made its appearance. The client would note the situation or circumstances that seemed to elicit the concern or the appearance of the subpersonality.

After gaining some insights into specific creative concerns or becoming aware of particularly influential subpersonalities as a result of doing the Evening Review, a person might very well make beneficial changes. The creative person might take more control of his subpersonalities or cope better with creative concerns.

For example, a creative might imagine putting a perfectionist subpersonality into a bottle with a tight lid or into a garden surrounded by a high wall so that the perfectionist wouldn't have any influence on the creative person while she was doing her creative work. On the other hand, a cheerleader subpersonality might be asked to stand close to the creative person as she was working, so as to provide encouragement and support.

 ## For Home Use

As I indicated earlier, this exercise is ideally suited for home use. Employ the instructions and adapt them to personalize the experience.

 ## Client Results

This exercise is relatively easy to do and yet can prove extremely effective. At almost the end of our session, George, a composer, groaned, saying, "I am supposed to compose several songs for a new movie being made, but I haven't been able to write a single note."

"What do you believe is the problem?" I asked.

"I don't know!"

"Well, since we're at the end of our session, how would it be if you did some homework?"

"What do you have in mind?"

I told him about the Evening Review, and he agreed to do it. The following week, he announced, "Now I know what's wrong. When I did that Evening Review for four days in a row, I discovered that I had filled almost every minute with some sort of social commitment. I didn't have any time or energy to compose anything!"

"So, what do you need?"

"I need to be alone! I'd like to be able to be a hermit—or at least live like one for a while."

"And can you do that?"

"You bet! I'm going to use a friend's cabin. He has a piano. I'll be all alone and I can work just as much as I want. I expect to get all the songs finished."

Sarah, another client, was having trouble getting any creating done. In our session, she was willing to try out the Evening Review exercise. Within a few minutes, she became aware of an aspect of herself that seemed to be heavy, lethargic, and sluggish. This part she imagined to be like a large, heavy sandbag.

When I asked her what she could do about this "sandbag," she said that she could cut a hole in the "sandbag," letting all the sand spill out. As she imagined doing just that, she seemed already more energetic. She agreed that someday she'd want to know more about this "sandbag," but for now she could use the Evening Review every night to make sure that the "sandbag" was no longer affecting her life.

* *

 About Marj Penley

Marj Penley's work is all about growth and expansion. For more than thirty years, she has worked with clients who have overcome limitations and expanded their abilities. Marj is a certified hypnotherapist, licensed therapist, and certified creativity coach. She also designs, creates, and sells her own ceramics, paints with watercolors, writes, and has published works on Collingwood's Theory of Art. She will soon have a book published on creativity. With techniques galore, Marj loves to support, guide, inspire, and empower people worldwide.

Marj welcomes email at marjpenley@gmail.com. More about her coaching, classes, and workshops can be found at her website, www.marjpenley.com.

Move Yourself! 22

Louise Lohmann Christensen

Exercise Purpose

This exercise helps artists move through resistance. When feeling resistance to working on your project or anxiety around your project, you are asked to enter the feeling instead of running away from the feeling and avoiding the work.

 Exercise Description

Give yourself at least 10 minutes for this exercise, more if you feel it necessary. You can do this exercise in a small space or a large space. You place yourself on the floor, preferably with bare feet or in shoes if you feel you must. You can close your eyes to begin with, if that makes it easier to access your inner world, but I do recommend doing this exercise with your eyes open as much as possible.

Notice your breathing and the feelings that are currently present. Then let those feelings move your body. The movement can be as small as moving your wrist or as large as jumping. You're letting the feelings express themselves through your limbs and other body parts. This is not dancing and there is no music playing, primarily because music dictates emotions and we are looking to express what is there, not produce new emotions.

You can move as slow or as fast, as soft or as hard, or as big or as small as you feel. I recommend that you do your best to let your body express your feelings without trying to control your movement by thinking about how you want to move. Just let it happen.

Moving this way may cause you to experience all kinds of feelings: joy, sadness, anger, and so on. Let them be felt and expressed in the movements. Sometimes it takes some minutes to let yourself relax into the movement, and that's natural and okay. If you have a timer set, you can move until it rings, or you can let the movement die out on its own accord. The more you engage with the exercise and move, the more you will be able to feel when the energy has been released and you can return to your creative work in a new state of mind. Don't worry if you sometimes feel the resistance or anxiety linger on, since you are not trying to get rid of it but rather to express it to see what happens next.

You can prepare for this exercise by writing about your thoughts, concerns, and feelings so that you already have a connection to them before you bring in the body. You can use the following questions: "What is it that makes me resistant to this creative task? What are the consequences if I do it or don't do it? What is it that I am trying not to feel or do?" You can continue to ask non-judgmental questions so as to go deeper into your subconscious.

 ## In Session or as Homework

In working with a client, you might have a conversation with her about the resistance and ask her to sit quietly breathing, noticing where the emotion is located in her body. You can ask her to breathe into that specific place in the body and ask her if the feeling has a physical expression and, if so, what it would look like. Then ask her to express it from where she is sitting or standing. It can be a series of movements or a single position or gesture expressed by her hands, her arms, or her whole body. You can invite her to do this before she begins the full 10-minute exercise. This will help her get comfortable connecting her body to her emotions. If she is having a hard time connecting her body to her feelings, you might ask her to just do a simple movement and then repeat it without stopping, letting it grow and transform into another movement, as repetition of any kind tends to reveal feelings. When she is done, you can chat with her about the experience and help her get even more comfortable with movement.

 ## For Home Use

This exercise is doable at home just as long as you have a little space to move around in. And if you don't have the space, if your home is full of things and there is absolutely no room for a bit of moving, you can still do the exercise sitting on the couch or lying in bed. There is not really a limit to moving the body in connection with emotion. We do it all the time in our everyday life; we just don't think about it. The unconscious moves us all the time. We turn away from people or situations we don't like, we walk closer to who we want to be nearer, we collapse when we are tired or sad, we tense our shoulders or our fists when we are angry or scared, and so on. By bringing consciousness into the process and by allowing yourself to be present to how your body wants to express emotion, you are allowing a new kind of processing to take place. This can begin to free you up, and you may discover new and provocative things about yourself.

Client Results

I have done this kind of work myself, trained alongside others, and shared experiences that have proven the importance of movement. It has been a direct way of channeling emotions that were too intense to hold in the body while sitting still. I've had times where I was anxious about an upcoming event or about meeting certain people, dared to give those feelings free expression through my body, and successfully transformed the emotions.

It has been scientifically proven that the primitive brain, where our fear responses are stored, does not respond to reason but rather to bodily sensations. Movement can release and restructure the way that we process feelings like anxiety and fear.

I worked for a while with a woman who was going through a lot: she was trying to raise a son without his father being present, she was struggling financially, she was holding onto a toxic relationship with an abusive boyfriend, she was wanting to sing in public but not daring to, and more. She felt stuck and also ashamed of her desires. While we were talking, it became clear that there was a little girl inside of her who was longing to be seen and who wanted to express herself. Eventually, I asked her if she wanted to dance and she replied "YES!" I let her jump and dance around the room while I talked to her and encouraged her to move exactly the way she wanted. I followed her with my attention so that she had a witness to her experience. When she finally stopped, she was smiling and beaming. This instant transformation occurred because she allowed her body to express what needed expressing.

**

 ## About Louise Lohmann Christensen

Louise Lohmann Christensen is a multi-artist, a trained actor (William Esper Studio), and a student of voice, having studied voice and movement with Patrick Michael Wickham, Ted Morin, and Celina Salver. Louise, who is also known as Kendra Lou (her recording name), has released two albums, *To the end of the world* and *Songs of the Black Moon*, plus many singles in collaboration with other artists. She has performed in Copenhagen, London, New York City, and Tucson and has created artworks shown at the Monsoon Art Collective and the Sculpture Resource Center in Tucson, Arizona.

Louise teaches acting as well as movement and coaches people in authenticity and creativity. Contact her at www.creativekobra.com or creativekobra@gmail.com.

Feeling Your Way to Creativity

23

Mary Ann Burrows

Exercise Purpose

The purpose of this exercise is to help connect us to the deep wisdom inside that speaks without words or thought and without limits.

 Exercise Description

Our body has its own built-in navigation system, always available to provide guidance as we go through life. It also helps us to create.

Everything that affects the mind also affects the body and everything that affects the body also affects the mind. They are one and the same.

We can use our body as a guide to help connect us to the deep wisdom inside that speaks without words or thought and without limits.

In Session and as Homework

I have used this exercise with clients as a life coach/creativity coach, and I've also used this on myself every day as a writer and artist. It has changed things dramatically for me in my own creative work and in my life.

You will need a pen and paper and a quiet spot to work in for approximately 10 minutes.

Step 1. Close your eyes.

Step 2. Pause and turn your attention to your body.

Step 3. Drop into pure awareness.

Step 4. Take a number of deep breaths in and out.

Step 5. Notice your breathing.

Step 6. Feel your feet on the floor.

Step 7. Bring a thought into your mind that is bothering you, one about your life or your creative work.

Step 8. Visualize the thought in your mind's eye. (The thought could be anything from feeling afraid to show your creative work, to feeling blocked or being unable to finish a project, to not knowing where to turn next.)

Step 9. With the thought in your mind and without judgment, calmly scan your entire body, observing your physical sensations.

Step 10. Ask yourself, "Where do I feel this issue in my body?" Do you feel it in your chest? Your stomach? Your heart?

Step 11. Describe the feeling in words. Does it make this area of your body feel heavy or light? Do you feel free and expansive or tight and constricted?

Step 12. Sitting in stillness, learn to listen to your body. Using the words that you came up with to describe your sensation, ask your sensation what it's trying to say to you. For instance: "Tight constrictive feeling, what are you trying to tell me?"

Step 13. Listen for the answer.

Step 14. Give the sensation voice and speak from that voice.

Learning to tap into your body can help you make creative decisions about what you should do next, what color you should use next, or in what direction you should take the project next. With a little practice and patience, this technique of tapping in can help you learn to identify your body's "YES" and "NO" sensations.

These sensations sit in the area of your mind that exists with your inner knowing and intuition. They are the greatest tool in your toolbox as an artist and as a human. Learning to tap into them through your body is a key to clearing the pathway.

To begin with you need to first find out how YES feels in your body and how NO feels.

Finding Your YES and NO

Step 1. Think of a day in your life when you felt on top of the world. You had made a good decision for yourself and your life was going in a positive way. Write down how you felt in your body that day. For example, YES might have felt like freedom or like happy butterflies in your stomach. This is your YES.

Step 2. Think about a day in your life when you were not having a good day, and things were not going well. Describe how you felt in your body. This is your NO. For example, NO might have felt like prison or like a dark pit bubbling in the bottom of your stomach.

Step 3. Sit with each of these feelings and scan your body. How does your body react when you are having a YES moment? How does your body react when you are having a NO moment? Write down what you're noticing and learning.

 For Home Use

You can bring this new body/mind awareness into your creative work and learn to trust your body as a guide, using it as another tool in your art studio, one that is ready and willing to *help you* make creative decisions.

Practice makes perfect. Sit still for a few minutes before you start to paint or write and tune into your body.

Pick up a tube of paint that you intend to use. Tune into your body and use it as a guide. Ask your body "Is this a YES?" Watch how your body reacts. Pick up another color and ask the same question. As you paint, stop at the crossroads, tune into your body, and ask yourself how you would feel if you took the painting in a certain direction. How does your body feel?

Grounding yourself with this yes/no exercise before you paint and as you paint will help you connect with the deeper wisdom inside you, and your inner voice will speak to you as you drop into your awareness. The answer lies within you.

We can use creative mind/body connection exercises in different areas of our lives as well. Be aware of how your body is reacting as you read your manuscript out loud or look at your finished piece of artwork. Observe, take note and write down how your body is feeling. Is it open and feeling delight? Inspired? Energized? Does it feel off? Your body will let you know. Taking a few moments to listen can save you time, anxiety, and stress down the road.

 Client Results

I have used this exercise successfully with both artists and non-artists. One client, Jane, had no idea that her mind and her creativity were connected to her body. She was exhausted from running a family, a business, and trying to become an artist. Her body was on an emotionally overloaded roller coaster. Once she tuned into her body and learned to listen to herself, she asked her sensations of stomach tightness and chest tightness what they were trying to tell her. She learned that she was exhausted and really needed a rest. She listened and rested. Her creativity came back full force once she allowed herself to take a break.

I have also had personal experience with this as a writer and a painter. I found that the more I practiced, the more aware I became of my sensations and the better it worked. Once I learned to trust the signals that my body was sending to me, it was easier for me to know when I was on the right path or the wrong path with a project, and I was able to change directions, if necessary, and waste less time. I was able to make decisions more quickly, and I found value in slowing down and tuning in to learn what direction to take next. Using this exercise increased the connection between myself and the deeper wisdom that speaks to me. My body will always let me know.

**

 About Mary Ann Burrows

Mary Ann Burrows is a visual artist, writer, and life/creativity coach. She especially loves writing and illustrating children's books. A spiritual adventurer since early childhood, her creative work is used for healing, meditation, connection, and astral journeying. She is a truth-seeker and a seer who coaches others in small workshops and one-on-one, helping them to meet their soul through creativity. Visit www.maryannburrows.com.

Tapping to Relieve Performance Anxiety

24

How to Rewire Your Nervous System and Affirm Self-Love and Self-Acceptance

Dwight McNair

Exercise Purpose

The purpose of this exercise, which employs EFT (Emotional Freedom Technique or "tapping"), is to greatly reduce and in most cases completely eliminate the feeling of stage fright (performance anxiety) by gently tapping on specific meridian points to stimulate the body's energy system and discharge blocked energy before a performance.

 ### Exercise Description

Step 1. On a scale from 1–10, with 10 being the highest level possible, have the client determine the level of anxiety that he or she is experiencing and assign it a number.

Step 2. Have the client announce whatever he or she is experiencing: for example, that her palms are sweating, her knees are shaking, her heart is "beating out of her chest," and so on.

Step 3. Have the client lightly tap with the fingertips of both hands on the top and center of the head (the crown) and say affirmatively: "Even though (whatever the circumstance or the situation is, for instance, that her palms are sweating and her knees are shaking), I DEEPLY and COMPLETELY LOVE and ACCEPT MYSELF."

Step 4. Move down to the outside of both eyes and tapping with the fingertips of both hands affirm: "Even though my palms are sweating and my knees are shaking, I DEEPLY and COMPLETELY LOVE and ACCEPT MYSELF."

Step 5. Move both hands to under the eyes and tapping with the fingertips repeat affirmatively: "Even though my palms are sweating and my knees are shaking, I DEEPLY and COMPLETELY LOVE and ACCEPT MYSELF."

Step 6. Move the dominant hand under the nose, tapping and affirming: "I DEEPLY and COMPLETELY LOVE and ACCEPT MYSELF."

Step 7. Move both hands to both collarbones, tapping and affirming: "I DEEPLY and COMPLETELY LOVE and ACCEPT MYSELF."

Step 8. Now, using one hand and then the other, turn the hand over and tap on the inside of the wrists, one at a time, affirming: "I DEEPLY and COMPLETELY LOVE and ACCEPT MYSELF."

Step 9. These steps complete one round of the procedure. Repeat it three more times.

Step 10. Now take several deep breaths, inhaling and exhaling completely. After the third round, scan your body and determine your level of anxiety using the 1–10 scale. Has the intensity gone up or down? If so, to what number? Has it remained the same? If any of these is the case, repeat the procedure until it drops to the point where you feel it is no longer an issue.

This exercise can also be done standing in front of a mirror. Look into the mirror and follow the instructions.

In Session or as Homework

This exercise can easily be used in session with the coach guiding the client through the steps. Perhaps you are working with a client who is experiencing performance anxiety that manifests as shortness of breath, an inability to walk out on stage, difficulties making important calls to marketplace players to ask for gigs, or problems confronting situations where their career could be advanced or jeopardized. In these types of situations, this technique has yielded wonderful results.

One of my clients, Samantha, was a pianist. Whenever she played publicly, her hands would actually tremble and shake so much that she was unable to play the piano without making multiple mistakes. So, we created a script that went as follows:

+ While tapping on the top of her head with the fingertips of both hands, she affirmed: "Even though I get so nervous before I play the piano in public that my hands shake uncontrollably, I deeply and completely love and accept myself."
+ While tapping on the sides of both eyes, she affirmed: "Even though I get so nervous before I play the piano in public that my hands shake uncontrollably, I deeply and completely love and accept myself."
+ While tapping under both eyes, she affirmed: "Even though I get so nervous before I play the piano in public that my hands shake uncontrollably, I deeply and completely love and accept myself."
+ While tapping under her nose, she affirmed: "Even though I get so nervous before I play the piano in public that my hands shake uncontrollably, I deeply and completely love and accept myself."
+ While tapping on both collarbones, she affirmed: "Even though I get so nervous before I play the piano in public that my hands shake uncontrollably, I deeply and completely love and accept myself."
+ While tapping on the inside of both wrists, she affirmed: "Even though I get so nervous before I play the piano in public that my hands shake uncontrollably, I deeply and completely love and accept myself."

After using this script, Samantha was able to approach playing the piano in public in an entirely different manner. Her nervousness significantly subsided and her hands stopped shaking, allowing her to play with far fewer mistakes.

 ## For Home Use

Let's take a situation where a coach has been working with a client who is afraid to promote himself in the marketplace. The client has decided that he needs to develop tools to assist him in building his confidence speaking and negotiating with club owners and managers. This is an ideal opportunity to use this exercise. You might help the client develop an EFT script to prepare him to, say, call five venue managers and discuss the possibility of securing a gig. The script sentence could be something like: "Even though I'm absolutely terrified to call the manager of Bethesda Jazz and Blues Club to get a gig, I deeply and completely love and accept myself," and the tapping would proceed as directed, with the client doing the work at home.

Client Results

I have used this exercise many times with a number of clients. Jason, for example, was literally unable to pick up the phone and make a call to club managers. He would panic and just hang up when someone answered the phone. But after guiding him through the EFT process using the script and having him practice at home, he was able to move forward and confidently interact with club managers and other marketplace players. The proof is in the pudding. Try it and see!

**

 ## About Dwight McNair

Dwight McNair is a singer/pianist/songwriter, vocal clinician, creativity coach, and author of *A Singer's Prayer and Meditation: A Spiritual Guide for Inspiration and Hope* and *25 Powerful Low or No Cost Things You Can Do NOW to Jump Start Your Singing or Instrumental Career*. He was an opening act for the legendary rhythm and blues singer Phyllis Hyman and has shared the stage with many notables, including jazz greats Barry Harris and Jon Hendricks of Lambert, Hendricks and Ross. He has performed nationally in the U.S., in Europe, Africa, and in Canada. He is the recipient of numerous awards, grants, and recognitions, among them a Fellowship to the Juilliard School of Music and the University of Ghana, where he did field studies in traditional African drumming, rhythm, and ritual. He currently operates a music studio in the Washington, DC area and is recording a new album to be released in 2020. He is also a certified yoga teacher and EFT (Emotional Freedom Technique) Practitioner. You can reach Dwight at dwightmcnair@icloud.com or dwightmcnair@aol.com or by phone at 202-486-3741.

The Sense Awareness Ritual **25**
How Mindfulness Helps You Create

Halli Bourne

Exercise Purpose

When imagination runs amok . . .

Among the many strengths we creative people possess is our ability to *imagine*. We can create whole worlds from overheard conversations, transform a familiar object into a fresh and surprising landscape, romanticize the changing of the seasons, and influence how we see ourselves through our creations.

The downside of this ability, however, is the tendency to catastrophize and imagine worst-case scenarios, which creates anxiety for ourselves and frustrates our work. If this happens when we're approaching a creative project, we can slide into judging ourselves for not measuring up, prioritizing the needs of others above our need to create, and so become consumed with indecision and apprehension.

 Exercise Description

This is about learning to pay attention.

When my mind gets hijacked by self-doubt, criticism, and perfectionism, I use this Sense Awareness Ritual to help me tune back into the present moment and find inspiration through the senses.

By shifting my awareness toward each of my physical sensations, I become less anxious and more focused on the simplicity of just paying attention. This lets me see familiar problems from a brand-new, expanded perspective, and I come out of the experience with a ravenous creativity.

I've also seen the power of this deceptively simple exercise in many of my clients' creative lives. By describing the steps in detail, I hope to bring this same ritual to everyone who's interested in learning it.

✿✿ In Session and as Homework

The Sense Awareness Ritual

Getting Ready

You can use this exercise as a preparation ritual any time you intend to create something. Start in the space where you'll be creating, and eliminate as many distractions as possible. Withdraw into a place you find soothing and safe, erecting an imaginary protective barrier between yourself and everything that's distracting you. The world and your responsibilities will always be there. Right now, you're making a decision to tune in and listen to your soul's call for creativity. Claim your role as a creator, and resolve to remove any obstacles in your way.

You can perform this exercise either sitting up or lying down. You can read through the ritual first and then take yourself through it, or you can record yourself describing the steps beforehand. Avoid any background music, since listening to the sounds in your environment is an important part of the ritual. It can be tempting to fuss over the details of setting up for this practice, but that's just a sneaky way to avoid being present, so watch out for this and commit yourself fully to this time.

Set up your workspace ahead of time so you can transition directly from this ritual into your creation.

How It's Done

Make yourself comfortable. Be still and quiet. Let go of any need to assess or analyze what you're experiencing. Be open and curious.

Take a long, slow, deep breath, and then let your eyes rove around the room as though you're seeing it for the first time. This approach is called *beginner's mind,* and invites you to suspend old ideas to make room for new ones. Take in everything that enters your visual field as your eyes move over and onto particular objects.

When an item's story begins to form in your head—where it came from, what significance it has for you, etc.—mentally drop the story and focus on its empirical qualities. What textures, colors, and shapes do you notice? Study this object until you've seen all that you can see, and then let your vision wander again. Notice where your eyes land next, tapping into the wonder of an explorer in a foreign place.

Shift your attention now to the sounds you can hear around you, maybe even the sound of your own breath. Notice how the mind wants to identify, judge, and react to these sounds. *Why do they always have to mow on Sunday morning?* or *I wish they'd keep that dog inside when they leave.* When you notice your mind creating a story from these sounds, try to drop the association and think of the sounds for what they are—mental feedback from vibrations in your eardrum. Maybe you can experience the sound as a physical sensation that you've never noticed before.

Notice what you smell, what you taste, what you feel against your skin. Then, moor your attention to the palms of your hands, tuning into all of their sensations. Linger here for a while, noticing all the pulsing energy and circulation that comes from being alive.

Now, take a few deep breaths and allow your eyes to open. Take in what's around you while still focusing on your hands. Breathe, feel, and look around, staying tethered to your body as you become aware of your external environment once more.

Take this moment to set an intention for your creative time, for example, "I resolve to release my self-doubt, criticism, and perfectionism and open to the flow of Source."

Take another deep breath, open yourself to inspiration, and go create.

 ## For Home Use

This exercise is ideally suited for home use. Simply follow the instructions, either as they are or modified to suit your style and purposes.

 ## Client Results

I use this ritual often when I'm sitting down to either write or paint, and I find that it helps me let all my worries and preoccupations recede, get out of my own way, and allow the forces of creation to do their thing. Anyone can do the same by just sitting down and trying it out.

Diane wanted to enter a short story competition, but she struggled with self-doubt every time she sat down to write. Whenever she did get something down, she would edit and re-edit the same passage until her writing was overworked and lifeless. She often felt overwhelmed by all her other obligations, which conflicted with her desire to write this story. When she came to work with me, she was considering retirement and wanted help prioritizing time to write.

She admitted feeling self-conscious when we first began, but I sensed that she was eager and hopeful to rein in her distracted mind and free her spirit's need to write. I guided her to close her eyes for a moment, and to shift out of thinking and into feeling—into *being*. I was surprised at how quickly she embraced the essence of the ritual. I watched tenderly as her eyes settled on an object across the room and quickly filled with tears. "So beautiful . . ." I heard her mutter.

When we completed the ritual together, she reported feeling clarity and internal softness, followed by a flood of ideas for how to complete her short story. Diane and I continued to work together, and she adopted the Sense Awareness Ritual as a way to make writing a part of her everyday life. In just two months, she had completed her story and started a second one. She was no longer controlled by her cynical imagination, and had instead learned to approach her creativity with enthusiasm, curiosity, and confidence. All it took was a little mindfulness.

* *

 ## About Halli Bourne

As a creativity and performance coach with more than thirty years' experience, Halli Bourne helps other creatives overcome issues of stage fright, performance anxiety, self-criticism, perfectionism, writer's block, and boredom to connect with what flows genuinely from the soul so as to bring their expression out into the world.

Halli's work as a coach involves a process of thought inquiry, focus, and awareness, otherwise known as mindfulness and witness consciousness. In Halli's words, "It is one thing to desire a creative life and another thing entirely to generate the optimal conditions for it to exist. The commitment to creativity is a decision to turn away from the world's incessant reverberations about who we *should* be and a turning *toward* an active-yet-quiet state of mind where our brains and hearts can unite in a soul-nourishing way."

Halli is a certified professional life coach and creativity coach. She is also a senior-level Kripalu yoga and meditation teacher, a mindfulness mentor, a freelance writer, a vocalist, a lyricist, a dancer, and a visual artist with a B.A. in theatre arts. Visit www.hallibourne.com.

Creative Boxes
26

Midori Evans

Exercise Purpose

Creative Boxes helps creatives organize and shape their creative working spaces.

 ## Exercise Description

How many of you wish you could walk in your house after a long day, relax for a bit, but then still have a chance to do some creative work? One of the biggest obstacles to that happening is that it feels as if there are too many steps standing between *being where we are* and *actively creating*.

For just a small investment of time and money, you can make stations in your house where the things you want to do live. Lots of art supply stores and home decor shops, such as Michael's or Home Goods, sell different sizes and designs of decorative boxes. With so many choices, something is sure to strike your fancy or fit in with your decor.

The boxes look elegant and can live in plain sight; the gift is that they hold the marvelous tools of creation. Pastels, your writing notes, unusual recipes, knitting needles and yarn . . . whatever your creative bent is, it can be stored in a box like this, easily placed, put away, or moved from room to room. You always know where your tools and your inspiration are.

You can grab them and go sit outside on the porch. Or the box lives in front of where you keep the TV remote, so that you have to consciously move your creative tools before accessing the TV remote. It's an individual decision how to make use of these boxes, but they are bound to help you better integrate your creative materials into your life.

In Session or as Homework

This exercise clearly works best if the client is in his or her own working or living environment. If you are planning on doing this exercise in session, make sure you address the topic in the first of two sessions so that boxes can be purchased ahead of time. Once the boxes are purchased, you can have an interactive activity during a phone or video conference call. Try asking questions like, "Where do you envision doing your painting?" or "Is there a room you are often in but that is too cluttered to be effective as a workspace?"

Then brainstorm together what else in the space might need to be removed, repurposed, or shifted. The entire time, the focus should be on making it as easy as possible to finish with: "Now, open that box and start to work!" If you are working on installing decorative boxes into a workspace, you might add in the element of how to keep the material in the decorative box specific to creative bursts, not allowing it to be just another substitute for an inbox. Is there a distinct shelf where it can live? Might there be a sign you put nearby to remind you that within the box are some of your best creative tools?

During the remote coaching session, your client can walk around the space, thinking through good places for the boxes to live, or sorting through and finding alternate homes for whatever clutter may be taking up a good creative workspace. If assigned as a homework assignment, it merely requires a slightly different approach versus being done in session. Integrating photographs into a homework assignment helps with the accountability piece. Ask your client to take photographs of the inside and outside of the boxes once they have found their new homes and send them to you by a specific date. Then watch the creating begin!

 ## For Home Use

At home, creatives can decide how to integrate their decorative boxes into their daily lives. You could have one decorative box in each room, let each family member be responsible for his or her own creative box, or make travel decorative boxes to take along with you on your business trips.

It's important to remember that it is so easy to name excuses, claiming not to have time for our creative projects. Creative Boxes reminds us that these projects are important to us and the boxes serve as antidotes to our excuses. In addition, Creative Boxes is not a one-time-only exercise. It can be revamped as often as needed in order to keep current projects accessible and ready to go.

 ## Client Results

Clients who have done this exercise express great glee at how simple it is and yet how remarkably effective. It does not require weeks of intervention or expensive classes—merely a small investment in design strategies. By helping clients identify their current creative project as well as both where and when they want to be working on that project, the struggle to *start* gets reduced. By paying attention to the client's environment and integrating creative goals into the workplace or home, a new felt sense of integration arises.

Clients have talked about how the boxes add a sense of mystery and deepen their creative practice. Rather than a haphazard pile of photo books, lens caps, and memory card readers, a photographer stands in front of his blue-sky fold-top box and thinks to himself, "A sunset is waiting." One friend who adopted this exercise told me that she chose only decorative boxes with pictures of exotic places on them. "I get to imagine myself in Paris or in Tokyo and it gets my creative juices flowing!"

The practicality of this exercise is multi-purpose. Even if you can't kick off your shoes the minute you walk in the door, you can still multi-task. One mother said, "I walked into the kitchen and all I could think about was wanting to open my watercolor box! It was such a great idea to put it near the refrigerator, as now I get out my paints and start mixing the colors before I grab the veggies to make a salad for the kids' dinner."

* *

 About Midori Evans

Midori Evans is the founder of Midori Creativity, a coaching and consulting business in Westport, Massachusetts, that helps artists and businesspeople manifest their creative visions. She is fascinated by how we both create meaning and become our true selves. An experienced teacher and coach, she explores the world through writing, photography, and solo travel. She has traveled to places as far-flung as Tunisia, Finland, and Japan and walked the Camino Frances through Spain. Midori Creativity offers private coaching, workshops, artist critique groups, and the Creativity Abloom conversation series. Visit midoricreativity.com, cedarlightimages.com, or email midori.creativity@gmail.com.

The Power of Visualization for Creative Focus **27**

Nick Lazaris

Exercise Purpose

This exercise helps creatives powerfully picture success while quieting the inner, negative voice that creates obstacles to doing their best work.

 Exercise Description

Creating a consistent and positive mindset, as the creative begins their work, is critical to success, whether in visual art, writing, or performing. The ability to stay focused, while quieting creative anxiety and fear of failure and rejection, is foundational if the world is going to have the opportunity to enjoy the fruits of their amazing talents.

A powerful technique to use in preparing for optimal performance as a creative is visualization. If one cannot imagine performing well in their creative endeavors, if they cannot 'see' in their mind's eye doing well, then they will have very little chance of actually creating outstanding work. This becomes especially true with the pressure that most creatives put themselves under. The more pressure they experience, the more important it is to imagine doing well as they create.

Here are five steps for practicing visualization for focused creativity:

Step 1. Create a Clear Intention

Ask yourself: What do I intend to achieve as a result of this exercise and in my time of creating?

Step 2. Take a Slow, Deep Focused Breath

Center yourself physically and mentally in order to slow down any anxiety or stress during visualization.

Step 3. Visualize in Your Mind What Your Intention Would Actually Look Like

Try to see, feel, and hear yourself creating powerful and moving work as you apply yourself to the creation in front of you.

Step 4. Attempt to Use All of Your Senses

Picture yourself being in a zone of creativity as you visualize using all your senses.

Step 5. Allow Yourself to Correct Your Mistakes

Even in visualization, you will discover that while mentally practicing you might visualize making a "mistake" with your creation or becoming afraid and anxious about being seen as an "imposter." "Stop the tape" and correct your pictured "mistake" until you can clearly see yourself calmer, more relaxed, and doing well in the moment.

 ## In Session or as Homework

Remind the client, as you are introducing the exercise, about the *power of mindset* in the creative process, how "getting out of your own way" is crucial to allowing the right-brain process of creative spontaneity to express itself.

Next, stress the importance of *setting a very clear intention* of exactly what they would like to accomplish as a result of utilizing visualization. For example, is their intention to let their creative self choose bold new colors to apply on the canvas, or use a medium for their altered art piece that others might never have envisioned working so well together? Is their intention to be in the moment, letting go of fear and anxiety, while being fully present in their studio as their inner, creative self takes charge?

Help the client focus on *breaking up their visualization* into small little pieces, i.e., see themself preparing to paint, then picture the next segment as they choose their colors, then as they apply the medium to their developing piece of art, etc. Picture each of these segments in their mind *as clearly as possible* as they are confidently creating.

Encourage them to visualize being in a zone of creativity, feeling the brush or pen in their hand, hearing themself as they become excited with how the work is coming together, listening to the positive words that others will say about their work, as though they created it just for them, and experiencing how great it feels to walk away from their studio knowing they did a great job!

For Home Use

Encourage a client that this exercise takes relatively little time to do and that its ultimate success at home or in the studio, while actually doing the work, is dependent on consistently practicing the steps of the exercise in order to get better and better at visualizing creating great work without fear or anxiety.

The key at home is to find a place and time with no distractions, using a deep, focused breath to begin quieting the mind and then giving themselves permission to see themselves doing great work.

The more that they practice at home, prior to actually doing the work, the more the creative will become able to enter a zone of creativity, thereby preparing themselves for when they actually begin their creative process. Their real-life work as a creative will continue to improve the more that they can "experience" (see, hear, and feel) outrageous creativity in their visualization. Adding this skill to their creative toolbox becomes a reminder that they can begin to fully take charge of the process of creating or performing at their absolute personal best.

 Client Results

My client Stella was a writer and illustrator. She came to my office in order to develop skills to push past what turned out to be self-imposed obstacles. A lack of confidence, as well as years of feeling like an "imposter" as a creative, had led to paralysis whenever she attempted to write and illustrate her children's book.

As she anticipated approaching her work, the negative, gremlin-like voices in her head created a picture in her mind of doing work that no one would appreciate or buy. The more she listened to those voices, the more anxiety she experienced and the more vivid her negative picture would become.

It was clear that in many ways Stella was actually "rehearsing" or visualizing a negative outcome to creating her work, leading to the anxiety that stopped her in her creative tracks. After discovering how negative self-talk escalated her anxiety and stifled her creative process, she began the daily process of learning to practice a positive visualization of doing well in her studio.

Beginning with Stella determining her intention for the exercise (i.e., to slow and quiet her thinking in order to manage anxiety and resistance), she became quite good at using focused breathing to center and become present in her time of creating. In her mind's eye, she saw herself becoming fearless and only focused upon letting her creative self write or illustrate. What others might think, or whether the work was or wasn't "just right," became thoughts that would easily be quieted and "let go of" as she became more proficient in her visualization process.

Stella explained, "I am beginning to shut the voice up that used to lead to picturing myself failing in my work." Anxiety, procrastination, and waiting for "just the right time" to create faded as Stella gave herself permission to be free in her creative process.

 About Nick Lazaris

As a performance psychologist and creativity coach, Dr. Nick Lazaris has specialized for thirty-eight years in helping creatives, performing artists, entrepreneurs, and business professionals overcome anxiety in their art-making, writing, public speaking, or performing. Dr. Nick coaches those who desire to increase their self-confidence, overcome fear, and create at or near their personal best. He is available for a limited amount of performance coaching via phone, Skype, Zoom, or in person. You can contact Dr. Nick at nick@drnicklazaris.com or go to www.drnicklazaris.com to receive your free Performance Anxiety Road Map.

The Sacred Spiral Mindful Drawing Exercise

28

Rosa Phoenix

Exercise Purpose

This intuitive drawing and writing exercise uses the ancient symbol of the spiral to mindfully bring embodied awareness to the concept of expansion and contraction, reaching outside oneself and going within oneself, to achieve centering and balance. This exercise will give you a greater sense of strength, focus, and purpose.

 Exercise Description

This exercise requires a crayon and paper (or the drawing or painting medium of your choice). You also need a pen and paper to write with. You do not need to have any drawing ability to do this exercise. You should be in a quiet environment without distractions. Allow 15 to 20 minutes to complete the exercise. (Tip: If you are doing the exercise for yourself, you may wish to audio record the instructions that follow, and then play back the recording.)

The first part of the exercise is a visualization meditation. Here is the meditation:

Sit in a comfortable position, close your eyes, and take a few calm, cleansing breaths.
Find your body's center, wherever that may be for you, and breathe into it with loving energy.
Feel your body expand and contract with each inhale and exhale as you breathe into your center.
Imagine a root spiraling down from your center, all the way to the very center of the Earth. This root makes a strong connection to the source of all life.
Breathe in, up through your root, the life force energy of the Earth, its cleansing, renewing, creative energy, into your center.
With each breath out, let go of what you don't need.
Take a few more breaths here, into your center, feeling life force energy radiating out to all parts of your body and beyond.

When you feel "filled up," open your eyes and bring your awareness back to your environment.

Next, it's time to do the drawing exercise. Follow the wisdom of Nature, using the sacred spiral, a form that is found throughout all of Nature, all throughout the Universe, from our DNA to our galaxy.

With the crayon, put a dot in the center of the paper, a dot to represent your center.

Now slowly, mindfully, draw a spiral from this center dot outward. Go in whichever direction you want; the direction doesn't matter.

Breathing. Growing. Expanding. Opening. Go out to the edge of your paper.

Next, take your pen and the other piece of paper and write, briefly completing the following prompts:

I am growing towards . . .
I am reaching for . . .
I am expanding to . . .
I am opening up to . . .

Now go back to the spiral you drew and this time, use the crayon to trace it from the outside going in toward the center.

Then write again, using the following prompts:

I am inviting in . . .
I am bringing close to me . . .
When I go within, I find . . .
When I center myself, I feel . . .

Consider what you've just learned and experienced and incorporate that new learning into your creativity practice.

In Session or as Homework

This exercise can be used in a workshop or class, in a one-on-one or group creativity coaching session, or at home. I have used the sacred spiral exercise in creative manifestation workshops with small groups. The exercise is the first activity of the workshop, and it helps participants to release the mundane concerns of their daily lives and prepare them for the deep inner exploration of the workshop.

The drawing aspect brings them into a creative and sensory state so that they become focused on the present moment. The writing aspect helps them to access their inner wisdom that resides within their center, and gain clarity on their true desires and intentions.

The wonderful thing about the sacred spiral exercise is that the spiral drawing makes a perfect centering meditation tool that can be used after you have completed the exercise.

To use the spiral drawing as a meditation tool, simply trace the spiral with a finger going in the direction that you want to go (inward or outward), and while you are doing that, meditate on your intention for reaching out or going within.

For homework, try establishing a regular meditation practice using the sacred spiral meditation tool. Use this meditation tool regularly over time to strengthen your sense of centeredness and focus.

 For Home Use

Experiment With Media

Artists may create variations on this exercise using a variety of media. For example, it would be wonderful to create a version in clay or plaster that could be used like a finger labyrinth. Use your imagination and create something personal that expresses your vision.

Expansion Meditation

Say that you want to grow or stretch yourself in some way. Maybe you want to make new connections, launch an initiative, go in a different direction with your art, or reach out beyond your comfort zone. Begin by getting centered. Find your body's center, and breathe into it. Place your finger on the spiral's center and slowly trace the spiral outward as you imagine pulling energy up from the Earth's center into your own center, filling you up, expanding with strength from within and reaching out beyond your skin.

Centering Meditation

Say you've been feeling scattered or distracted by the myriad demands of everyday life. It's time to focus and do your work. Position your finger on the outside end of the spiral, and slowly and mindfully trace the spiral inward, toward the center. As you do this, bring your attention and awareness deep into your body, focusing on your center and breathing into it.

 Client Results

I have used the sacred spiral exercise with clients as a tool for them to gain clarity on their true desires and intentions for what they wish to create in their lives.

One client, a collage artist, said that it reminded her of walking a labyrinth. Another client, a screenwriter and novelist, told me that it brought her to divine connection. She also enjoyed the kinesthetic, sensory aspect, and the sense of childlike play that drawing with crayons evoked. For this client, the sacred spiral has become an important part of her regular prayer and meditation practice.

For both clients, the sacred spiral exercise connected them with their spiritual essence and allowed them to access their inner guidance.

I regularly use the sacred spiral as a meditation tool, by tracing my finger over the spiral I created. Over time I have discovered some insights. I realized that before I discovered this tool, I often reached outside of myself to escape or avoid the feelings or thoughts within. And also, that often when I went within, I was actually hiding from the outside world.

Since I began using the sacred spiral exercise, I have found strength within my center. Now when I seek to go within or reach out, it is not to escape or hide. Rather, my actions are based on conscious motivations that I have identified in the writing part of the exercise. I am operating with intention, from a place of purposeful strength and confidence.

** **

 ## About Rosa Phoenix

Rosa Phoenix is a visual artist, art teacher, and creativity coach, guiding people on a transformative journey to discover their own creative potential and the healing powers of the creative process. Her approach is intuitive and mindfulness-based, frequently blending visual art activities with other art forms like writing and music, and body-centered practices like yoga, breath work, and gentle movement. She offers classes, workshops, retreat facilitation, and one-on-one coaching. She is based in Portland, Oregon. To learn more, please visit www.rosaphoenix.com.

Into the Scene   **29**

Nefeli Soteriou

Exercise Purpose

This is an exercise specifically tailored to filmmakers. It helps filmmakers find solutions to creative problems through a hands-on exploration of the film's mise en scene elements ("mise en scene" is French for "placing on stage" and refers to the arrangement of everything that appears in the frame). Clients go beyond their everyday limitations to find new possibilities and expand their creativity.

 Exercise Description

The basic set-up for this exercise is as follows:

+ The client works on various scenes from his or her screenplay or screenplay-in-progress.
+ The client completes the exercise alone, without crew assistance.
+ The client keeps a process log that records his or her implementation structure and action steps from start to finish.
+ The client doesn't spend more than $20 on expenses associated with this exercise.
+ The coach provides a printed copy of the following steps and advises the filmmaker to try to complete the exercise within a two-week period, with one-week leeway given.
+ The coach may also assign each section of the exercise separately.

The exercise comprises four parts.

1. Staging: Movement and Acting

Pick a character from your newly finished screenplay or from one in the works and select a short-length dialogue or monologue, 2 to 3 minutes tops.

Find a quiet room and set a camera on a tripod. Dress up for the role. Should you need to visit your local thrift store to find clothes in advance, do so. Add some make-up. Rehearse the lines. Set the lens to a wide angle. Work through blocking your movement in and out of the camera frame. Record your performances, select your finest one, and describe for yourself what you've learned, using your process log to record your thoughts.

2. Setting

Buy a sheet of watercolor paper, A4, 8.27 x 11.69 inches or larger, and some watercolor pencils or watercolor paints. With a pencil, draw in detail the set of one pre-selected scene from your screenplay, including furniture, windows, wall decor, shelves, curtains, carpet, and props.

Use the One Point Perspective technique to make the drawing. Provided next are beginner's instructions for drawing a square with One Point Perspective. Research this technique further at a library or online, should you need further assistance.

One Point Perspective of a Square

1. Place your paper in the horizontal direction.
2. Draw a horizon line in the middle of your paper. The horizon line is a horizontal line that will represent the eye level in the scene.
3. Place a vanishing point anywhere on the horizon line. The vanishing point can be a dot or a small letter "x."
4. Draw the sides of a square box below the horizontal line.
5. Connect the appropriate corners to the vanishing point.
6. Congrats, you've successfully created a three-dimensional square!

Imagine where the light enters the scene and try to re-create it using your paints, painting the brightness and the shadows and thinking about the overall mood you want to convey in your scene. If you gently erase paint with a wet tissue, you can increase the brightness. Should you need more guidance, research watercolor techniques at the library or watch videos online. Record your thoughts and your results in your process log.

3. Costume and Make-up

With the opening scene of your screenplay in mind, spend some time contemplating the clothing and make-up that best suit your film's stylistic approach. For inspiration, check out fashion magazines, search the web, watch other films, visit costume rental houses, or gaze into clothing store windows. Pay a visit to your local thrift store.

Try out different costumes, check yourself in the mirror, and take some photographs with your smartphone. You might also chat with stylists at the make-up departments of the larger department stores, describe the appearance you want to communicate to your audience, and take a make-up demonstration. Document the results with more snapshots and record your results and your thoughts in your process log.

4. Cinematography

Move two light sources, for example your basic 500w Lowel lights, around a furnished room so as to light the room in a Film Noir way. (Film Noir is a stylistic approach in filmmaking that emerged in the 1940s. Typically, a black-and-white, high-contrast tonality stands out and is created by a "harsh" lighting set-up. Films in this style include *Stranger on the Third Floor* [1940] and *The Maltese Falcon* [1941].) Use household items, such as socks, foil, and white paper, to achieve this effect. Take still photographs to document the outcome and record your results and your thoughts in your process log.

 ## In Session or as Homework

The coach assigns the exercise as homework. Here are some questions that the coach can ask during a follow-up session:

1. How was the experience for you?
2. What inspiration or insight did you gain from engaging with the exercise?
3. In what ways can what you learned be implemented in your film?

 ## For Home Use

The client will likely tackle this exercise at home, as that is easiest and most cost-effective, but he or she may also use a friend's space or any other space that is available and that makes sense to use.

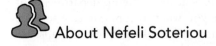 ## Client Results

After completing the exercise, one filmmaker shared how sticking to the limited budget of $20 taught him to better appreciate his own skills and resources. As a result, he dropped his vision of making a film with high-end production values and made a film within his means. Other clients have expressed how the exercise helped them better understand the complexity of filmmaking production and the need to push themselves to create a clear, sensible pre-production plan.

**

About Nefeli Soteriou

Nefeli Soteriou loves nature, exercise, and self-expression through art, adores animals, is interested in integrative medicine, produces indie narrative films and photography projects, holds an M.F.A. in Film and Media Arts, and is a Creativity Coach, an NYS Holistic Counselor, and an Energy Healer. If you'd like to learn more about Nefeli's work as a coach, visit www.nefelisoteriou.com.

Art-Making

Sacred But Nothing Special

30

Sasha Boyle

Exercise Purpose

This exercise will help you transition into a creative space and a creative mindset by temporarily pausing stresses produced by your current circumstances. Issues such as anxiety from poverty, concurrent life crises, and second career issues have the potential to act as a barrier between you and your creative practice.

 ### Exercise Description

Acute and/or prolonged exposure to stress can disconnect us from ourselves by shortening our attention span and muddying our mental clarity. This stress can easily start habits like obsessive worrying or constant shallow breathing, both of which are hard to break and have little benefit.

The goal is to encourage a daily art practice and to reframe art-making as, rather than a far-off, sacred but unattainable dream, an activity of everyday life that is so common that it becomes "nothing special."

In Session or as Homework

You will need low-stick painters' tape, two pieces of paper, and a pen.

Step 1. When will you create? Commit to a block of time for your creative practice. Write down the date and time of your commitment in your planner and honor it.

Step 2. What space will you be creating in? Using your low-stick painters' tape, make a box on the floor to define that space. It could be a small circle around a chair, a big square around a table, or a line at a doorway that symbolizes a threshold.

Step 3. Set a timer and put your mobile phone on its "Do Not Disturb" function (the quarter moon icon on iPhones). If you need to let people have a means of reaching you for a genuine emergency, you can let critical contacts (like caregivers who are covering for you) know that your phone is on DND and, if an emergency arises, they can call the number twice in a row. This will make the phone ring.

Step 4. On a piece of paper (paper A), write down the *one* (only one) creative thing you would like to do right now. Be as specific and simple as possible.

Step 5. On the other piece of paper (paper B), write down any worries that came up for you as you engaged with Step 4.

Step 6. Place and leave paper B outside of the threshold or barrier you created with the tape. Know that you will be back to collect this sheet of paper at some point, but for now it is safely waiting outside and you can forget about it.

Step 7. With paper A in hand, take a long, deep abdominal breath through your nose and enter the threshold you have created with the tape. Your only task is to work on this one item on paper A until the timer rings. *You've got this!*

Step 8. When your timer rings and it is time to leave your creative space, take a deep breath and step over your barrier, rejoining your community.

Step 9 (optional but recommended). Pick up your list of concerns, paper B. Cross out the issues that are beyond your control. Break down the remaining items on your list into manageable action items and calendar them. Honor your calendar.

 ## For Home Use

When you do this exercise the first time, you may find some resistance in transitioning back into non-creative time, picking up your list of concerns and returning to life as we know it. I would recommend creating a personalized exit ritual incorporating your olfactory system. Consider shopping for and picking a scent that triggers a positive memory of community and connection for you.

If nothing springs to mind, create your own association. What experience with joining a group has been very positive for you? Select an essential oil, candle, or object (e.g., a flower, plant, herb, exotic wood, or material) and smell that while you are mindfully contemplating that activity.

A few days later, repeat this exercise of recalling the scent and feeling its energy connection. Now, once your olfactory system has made that connection, smell that scent as you transition out of your creative mindset (Step 8).

If you continue to have trouble re-entering your creative space and your creative mindset, consider adding a short, 5-minute round of the yoga sequence sun salutation before your creative work (after Step 3 and before Step 4). This physical activity works wonders for clarity and stress reduction and can be adjusted to meet you wherever you are physically.

 ## Client Results

To take one example, Sam, a survivor of a coercive and controlling relationship (like four in ten women and four in ten men, who, according to recent studies, have experienced at least one coercive and controlling intimate relationship in their lifetime), experienced an erosion of her own personal perspective because of her relationship trauma.

She wanted to create art and reconnect with her muse and artistic identity, but when she finally arrived at the easel she found herself overwhelmed by feelings of panic and worry. This caused rapid, shallow breathing, which then affected her attention span, fogged her mind, caused her to lose clarity around her intention to make art, and eventually stopped her art-making altogether.

When an artist cannot find enough peace of mind to practice her craft in a particular place, she suffers a loss of an inner homecoming. An inability to focus on art-making for too long creates an experience of loss of creative peace and internal freedom. This creativity exercise is intended to aid artists, like Sam, who are having trouble returning to their creative space.

**

 ## About Sasha Boyle

Sasha Boyle offers a free download of a guided sun salutation audio on her podcast Sun Salutation + Saturn, which can be found on iTunes (https://podcasts.apple.com/us/podcast/cosmic-kitchen-sink/id1429282987?mt=2) or Libsyn (http://cosmickitchensink.libsyn.com). You can learn more about Sasha at www.sashaboyle.com.

Just Five Words

31

Nancy Johnston

Exercise Purpose

The purpose of this exercise is to help creatives who are working on writing projects reconnect with their projects and make small steps toward restarting or kickstarting the writing
process. It will also support creative people who identify as inexperienced writers or non-
writers. It can also be adapted for use with creatives in all the disciplines.

 Exercise Description

This is an idea-generating exercise that promotes "out loud" thinking and pre-writing.
The creativity coach will need a few materials: scrap paper (or cue cards or stickies), a
pad of paper, and pens or pencils. The coach will encourage the creative to work on paper,
if there are no mobility concerns, as this may help avoid fears associated with the blank
screen. The creative is invited to work in incremental steps: to think of ideas, to print or
write key words, to talk about their ideas, and finally to write.

The coach begins by asking the creative to do a relatively low-stakes task: to identify
five words related to their project. A coach might prompt with the following sorts of
questions:

+ What five words (or phrases) does your project need?
+ What five words (or phrases) do you want in the title of your project?
+ What five words (or phrases) are essential to include in an imaginary advertisement for
    your gallery show, book launch, or musical performance?

Creatives are given 5 minutes for the preliminary task and are invited to print or write
large. Alternatively, the coach might suggest that the creative circle or underline five words
in a draft or in some other project.

The next step is to ask the creative to talk about the five words and their connections to
each other. While their thoughts about possible connections are fresh in their minds, I typically will ask my client to arrange the words in a mind-map or to brainstorm about them.

The final step is to prompt a list of sentences using these words. The five words are
building blocks that they can use to get ideas out on paper and to see concrete progress in
their writing process.

In Session and as Homework

These techniques work well with visual learners and with creatives who might not currently describe themselves as successful or confident.

Most creatives are asked to write artist statements, apply for grant proposals, participate in reviews, etc. If an artist is working at home on such a task, he or she might try this exercise as a daily timed exercise or as a daily beginning activity.

 ## For Home Use

Some artists have tried using different media, such as painting the words into artwork or writing them separately on pages of an art journal as prompts. This exercise can be used at any point when the writing process feels stalled or overwhelming. In the middle of a project, the creative might identify key terms in a draft paragraph to help clarify the direction of the work-in-progress.

Client Results

Mel had been accepted into a prestigious group art show. She acknowledged it was an opportunity to showcase her new work and meet other local artists. However, she felt stuck when she started writing her artist statement, which only needed to be a short 250-word statement about her work. Although it was only to be a short statement, the task felt daunting to her.

"I'm not a writer," she said. "I know my work, that's not the problem. I'm just not confident in how I express what my work's about. What if I make myself look foolish?"

She always disliked writing essays in college and preferred visual expression. To enter the group show, she had written about her artwork and submitted her work. Now that she was accepted, writing the short statement felt derailing. I suggested that maybe her written application might be a good place to begin. I asked her to quickly circle all the essential words or phrases that she liked.

"What words—single words or very short phrases only—jump out at you? Don't evaluate them, rather claim them. And if the words you need aren't there, are there maybe other words that you need in your artist statement?"

Mel marked up her page and circled repeated words and terms: *bronze, sculpture, history, body, space.* I asked her to own these words and explain why they seemed important. After a short explanation, I suggested she write briefly or map the connections visually between them.

"How do some of these words fit together? Can you link two terms, as you would in a mind-map branch?" She began placing words together in pairs. I suggested she might give herself prompts or ask more questions.

Mel added verbs and wrote down new, simple sentences using some of her original words. I suggested that she might continue this work in a draft artist statement.

For her "homework," I suggested that she try using the following sentence stems:

+ I make [sculpture] . . .
+ I work with this medium [sculpture] to express how [the body] . . .

+ My work explores [the body/space] . . .
+ I am interested in ideas about [space] and [history] because . . .
+ In my work, I examine how [history] . . .

Mel finished her short artist statement in time to make her deadline. She didn't claim that she now felt more confident as a writer, but she was happy with her progress and her statement. She liked playing with her words and suggested that they were also touchstones that could help her prepare for talking about her work on opening night.

**

 About Nancy Johnston

Nancy Johnston is a writer, teacher, textile artist, and writing coach living in Toronto. She teaches writing and courses in gender and disability studies at the University of Toronto Scarborough, where she also works with instructors and students on academic writing. Her creative passions include facilitating workshops on writing and textile art for expressive and restorative play.

The Creative Zone

32

Stephanie Christie

Exercise Purpose

The purpose of this exercise is to help blocked creatives get back into the creative zone and to do so regularly.

 Exercise Description

Being creative is vital for many of us, but life can get in the way. After a change or during a busy time, it's common for creatives to stop creating and to then find it difficult to return to it. The four steps of this exercise will help you or your client create consistently again, even without a project in mind or a deadline looming.

We often blame a lack of time for not creating, but this usually isn't the main problem. More often it's a subconscious sense that creativity is too demanding. When we're stuck, we may be nostalgic for our memory of feeling creatively 'on fire' or working at a high level. However, this can set unrealistic expectations that only feed our avoidance of the creative space. To counteract this, we need to make getting to our creative practice as easy as possible.

I experienced this when I had a child. Parenting took so much energy! But I still needed to write poetry to be happy and functional. I carved out a regular creative time, so that I could take action immediately, trusting that inspiration and motivation would follow. You (or your client) can do this too, in under an hour, by following these four simple steps.

Step 1: Choose a Regular Time. When you're creating regularly, you can often snap into the creative work mode without needing to set aside any specific time. But if you aren't creating regularly, you will benefit from setting aside a regular time to be creative. Think about whether it will be daily, several days a week, weekly, or some other routine, and what time of day suits your creativity best. You may want to have a back-up time in case you miss the first one.

It helps to resist the urge to tell yourself that you'll do a big chunk of creative time. Small chunks are more likely to actually get done on any given day. Ten minutes can often turn into an hour, and 10 minutes is always a lot more than zero. Looking at your calendar will help you to identify available times (including activities you might be willing to let go of). To protect this time, you may need to set some boundaries, or use the magic word, "No."

Step 2: Choose What to Make. Reconnecting with the joy of creating is a brilliant way to overcome your blocks. After a creative gap, it can feel like you're back at the beginning, so it helps to start with a playful part of your creative practice. For example, if you have a graphic novel you want to write, you can start with sketching your cat! Lowering the stakes makes it much more likely that you'll actually do it.

It also helps to list "off-day options," low-key activities that support your creative practice, for when you feel out of sorts. This lets you turn up and keep the habit going, whatever your mood. You might want to consider your choice of materials too, and pick things that are easy to set up.

Step 3: Choose How to Start. To actively shift into the creative zone, get your subconscious on board. An easy way to do this is by starting with a ritual, a trigger, or a lead-in activity that you use every time. It could be lighting a candle, making a cup of tea, meditating, or going to a certain place . . . whatever resonates with you.

As the time to create nears, it often helps to focus on getting ready, instead of focusing on either your desires or on any fears around creating. You just go to your workspace, get out your materials, and do your starting activity. Then—BAM! Before you've had time to invent an excuse, you've started. This is a simple way to sidestep resistance.

Step 4: Choose How You'll Manage Your Mindset. Many of the biggest challenges in our creative lives are right here in our heads. Luckily, there are lots of skills you can develop that will help. I highly recommend learning ways to work with your inner critic (I love helping clients with practical strategies for this).

Journaling is a simple way to work with what comes up as you get creative again, if you experience off-putting thoughts or feelings. To build your motivation, you might like to pay attention to the meaningfulness that creating brings, in the moment and in the rest of your day. You could even write an encouraging mantra for your wall in your best felt-tip pens!

In Session and as Homework

To prepare a client for the exercise, I explain each of the steps and why they are important. My philosophy is that the "self" making the plan isn't always the "self" who has to carry it out. Each step helps a client visualize the future in detail, creating a practical plan and lessening your client's anxiety.

It helps to check in with clients to see what is working. It is very common for clients to build up ideas of what they "should" do, which then get in the way of them doing anything! If after a month this exercise isn't working yet, I move through the steps again with the client to troubleshoot what's gone wrong. It usually only takes a small adjustment to get the habit reestablished.

For Home Use

This is an exercise you can do for yourself right now. Get a piece of paper or whatever you like to use to record your ideas. Start with a brainstorming and journaling process for each step.

For example, for Step 1, put down the times that you can see could work for your regular creative time. You can write pros and cons, what would need to happen for this to work, and so on. If you get stuck, write out what's in your head (perhaps starting with a question to focus you) until you gain some clarity.

For each step, keep going until you have a clear idea of what you intend to do. Then, to make sure it sticks, write out a good copy of what you've decided on, perhaps even a beautiful one that you can put on your wall! This is a great way to keep your intention in the front of your mind, as the creative time you've chosen approaches.

To give "future you" extra support, put your chosen times in your calendar system. Make an action list if you need one. For example, such a list might include asking a friend to pick up the kids on Friday afternoons, buying new watercolor paper, choosing a notebook to collect your thoughts, fears, and observations, and so on.

You may find that a sudden change in circumstances knocks you out of your new creative habit. If this happens, it's okay. You can start over again whenever you're ready. You can visualize this routine as something solid that you're stepping back into, however long it's been since you've been away from it.

 ## Client Results

One of my clients was struggling to create because she couldn't choose what to work on. Photography, her big love, seemed overwhelming. Once we identified this as the cause of her block, she started creating daily with macramé. Within a week, she sent me a shot of her workspace: developing photos hung off every surface. Once she allowed her creative self to get into action, inspiration was able to get a word in.

Another client had a passion for painting and an extremely busy job. She was also very hard on herself, and her exacting standards clashed with what she was able to do in the 30 minutes per week she decided she could spare for her creative life. In Step 2, she set herself the task of drawing from life. After a couple of months, she began to struggle to show up for her creative time.

We checked in on each of the steps. She revealed that she'd chosen drawing because it was something hard that she thought "all real artists ought to be able to do"! We tweaked her activity so that it focused instead on playful experimentation with paint. She instantly found this fun and motivating. Through this process she also identified a mindset challenge—her perfectionist thought patterns—that she began to address.

Both clients came to me complaining that they were unhappy because they "didn't have time" for creativity. Now they are both creating regularly again. Having a set creative time is an easy way to bring satisfaction back into your creative life.

 ## About Stephanie Christie

Stephanie Christie is a poet and creative coach living in New Zealand. Her mission is to help creative people lead awesome lives. She believes creativity can be easy—or at least only as hard as the creative challenges you choose for yourself. She'd love to hear from you at www.stephaniechristiecreative.com or on Facebook and Instagram at @stephaniechristiecreative. If you want bespoke help to get back into the creative flow zone, get in touch!

The ABCDEFG Model

33

Niki Anandi Koulouri

Exercise Purpose

This journaling exercise, based on Albert Ellis's ABC model, can help creatives work through the process of ABCDEFG questioning and help them challenge themselves by disputing negative self-talk. Doing this enables them to feel better and manage their unhealthy emotions (depression, anxiety, anger, etc.), become aware of their maladaptive behaviors (procrastination, addictive behaviors, etc.), and respond to situations in a more helpful and productive way instead of simply reacting.

As creatives, we are often flooded with negative emotions such as anger, fear, shame, envy, and guilt, which hinder and block our creativity and quite often leave us feeling too blocked to create. Behind our unhelpful emotions and procrastination lie our negative thoughts and beliefs about ourselves, our art, and our relationships with others. It is important that the creator who wants to lead a conscious life, one with meaning and purpose and that serves her talents and creativity, develops her ability to "catch herself in action" and observe her thoughts, attitudes, and behaviors so as to gain awareness and develop her ability to change.

 Exercise Description

One tool that can help creatives on this path of self-awareness and self-management is the ABCDEFG model, based on the ABC model. The ABC model was developed by the psychologist and psychotherapist Dr. Albert Ellis, who was influenced by the Stoic philosophers and who developed rational emotive behavior therapy (REBT). REBT is both a philosophy and a system of psychotherapy, helping clients minimize emotional disturbances, decrease self-defeating behaviors, and become happier.

According to both the Stoic philosophers and Ellis, it's not adversity per se that causes our suffering but rather the beliefs we hold about what's happening. In this view, events are "neutral" and what colors the events are the thoughts and beliefs that we hold. The fewer "irrational" beliefs that we hold, the more we can live a life of harmony and joy. In Ellis's ABC model of emotional disturbance, A refers to an Activating Event or some Adversity, B refers to the Beliefs we hold, which are often irrational as we interpret events incorrectly or unrealistically, and C refers to the Consequences, both emotional and behavioral.

❂❂❂ In Session and as Homework

The ABCDEFG Journaling Exercise

Whenever an event occurs that leads us to irrational or distorted thinking and unhelpful emotions and behaviors, we can engage with the following journaling exercise using an ABCDEFG model. Here the letters stand for:

+ A. Activating Event/Adversity—What happened?
+ B. Beliefs—What did I think?
+ C. Consequences—What did I feel? What did I do?
+ D. Dispute Our Beliefs—How can I challenge them?
+ E. Effective New Beliefs—What new approach can I take?
+ F. Feelings—How do I feel right now?
+ G. Goal/New Plan—What is the goal? What is the new plan?

Let's look at some examples of how we can dispute our self-defeating beliefs and negative self-talk and transform them into effective new beliefs or enhancing thoughts:

Example 1: "I cannot produce a piece of writing as good as X" can be transformed into "Everyone has their own talent and writing style. I can finish my book if I give it a chance."
Example 2: "I can't do it well enough" can be transformed into "I can do it as well as I possibly can, and then I'll ask for feedback on how to improve things."
Example 3: "Others can do it better than I can" can be transformed into "It's no use thinking that others can do it better. What's the point of this useless thought?"
Example 4: "It's really hard for me to finish this project. I'm getting really stressed, and it's better that I give up. Besides, my art will not help me survive financially. And I will never be accepted or acknowledged by the art community." All of these thoughts can be transformed into "Yes, this is a real challenge for me, but I choose to do the best I can, as this is what I really want. There are colleagues who can make a living from their art, and I can join them. My peers will understand my work, and this is what I want to do; this is what makes me happy."
Example 5: "I'm bound to fail" can be transformed into "I won't know what will happen if I don't make the effort. With a good plan, clear focus, and a positive attitude, I can do it. I just need to figure out what will help me stick to my plan."

Seven Steps to Mastering the ABCDEFG Journal Method

Step 1. Activating event. Identify what event triggered the distorted thinking and clearly hear and identify the thoughts themselves.

Step 2. Beliefs. What do these thoughts tell me about what I seem to be believing? What are my hindering or unwanted beliefs?

Step 3. Consequences. What emotions are emerging and/or what behaviors are flowing from these thoughts, beliefs, and feelings?

Step 4. Dispute. Is it really true what I am thinking? What evidence is there to support my beliefs? What is my reaction every time I think this way? What would happen if I think differently?

Step 5. Effective new beliefs. I am writing down in as much detail as I can my new thoughts, my new beliefs, the new approaches I mean to take, and the new attitudes I mean to hold.

Step 6. Feelings. I am writing down the feelings that are emerging from me thinking new thoughts, holding new beliefs, and taking a new approach.

Step 7. Goals. What are my new goals? What is my action plan? What will I do to implement this action plan? What personal resources will I use? What external resources will I use? Where can I ask for help? What can prevent me from implementing my action plan? How can I manage it and how can I monitor it?

 ## For Home Use

This exercise is perfect for home use. The detailed instructions can be used as is or altered to fit your circumstances, issues, and style.

 ## Client Results

Coaches can use this exercise with their clients in all sorts of ways, explaining to clients that they will naturally go back and forth among these steps and that the process is not as linear or straightforward as the exercise portrays it to be. This is a genuine process of self-inquiry that will bring up powerful feelings, but a process that is well worth the effort and that can help clients move from distorted or irrational thinking to a mindset that serves them and their creativity far better.

 **

 ## About Niki Anandi Koulouri

Niki Anandi Koulouri is a certified trainer and coach with a broad portfolio of clients including entrepreneurs, executive leaders, and artists. She is a member of the European Mentoring Coaching Council (EMCC), Creativity Coaching Association, and the International Enneagram Association.

As a coach, she helps clients use their potential, creativity, and talents; live a conscious life with meaning, purpose, and joy; and achieve their goals. You can find out more about Niki Anandi and her work at www.nikikoulouri.com and www.4peoplematters.com or contact her at anandi@nikikoulouri.com.

Ambition Without Grandiosity

34

Rahti Gorfien

Exercise Purpose

This exercise is designed to help creatives distinguish ambition from grandiosity and separate out what matters to them from who they think they need to be, thus strengthening their ability to pursue the work.

 Exercise Description

Ambition Without Grandiosity is a journaling exercise that helps creatives better understand why ambition is a good thing, as it helps us persist even after failures. At the same time, it helps creatives understand why ambition coupled with grandiosity leads to shameful feelings and perfectionistic tendencies. If we are ambitious but not grandiose, we have access to the tenacity needed to proceed and eventually succeed.

Step 1. Study the Following Definitions

Grandiosity: An exaggerated belief in one's importance and entitlement masking feelings of extreme unimportance and unworthiness.

Ambition: An earnest desire for some type of achievement or distinction. It could be power, honor, excellence, fame, or wealth, and includes a willingness to strive for its attainment.

Step 2. Identify Your Segovia Complex

Andres Segovia was such a consummate guitarist that they named a complex after him. It is a mindset by which we view success in such black-and-white terms that we stop before we begin: "If I can't play like Segovia, I may as well not play at all."

Grandiose artists may start to build a career, but they are miserable because they secretly have a version of Segovia Complex going on in their mind. They *must* attain a certain level of greatness on a par with so-and-so for their journey to have been worth something at all. And if they do not reach that level of greatness, it only proves their inherent worthlessness.

So, first, who is your Segovia? For me, as a young actress, it was Meryl Streep. If this resonates with you, pick someone you feel you must live up to in order to feel successful. Next, write out everything that's positive about aspiring to be like them. Next, what's bad about aspiring to be like them? Finally, what conclusions can you draw from this analysis? These are your "takeaways." You can do this in the form of a table or a list. Mine looks like this:

Meryl Streep:
Good: Impeccable professional. Aggressive and tenacious. Rich and famous with great boundaries.
Bad: Many people are jealous of her and are hypocritical when they speak about her. My own jealousy has kept me from being happy and making the most of who I am.
My Takeaways: Meryl Streep's success is not at my expense. And, if I get well-known and respected, there will be people who don't like me for it.

Step 3. Failing and Persisting

Ambition in the absence of grandiosity allows us to fail and persist. Failure allows us to learn, and if it is not the occasion for shame due to grandiosity/perfectionism (flip side of the same coin), then we have access to the tenacity needed to proceed and eventually succeed! This next step is meant to help you parse out your true ambitions from what may be grandiose fantasies.

Use the following questions as journaling prompts:

+ What does it mean to succeed at something?
+ Where and when has grandiosity stopped you from achieving something?
+ What do you want badly enough to fail at repeatedly (aka suck at)?
+ What is worth doing whether you succeed at it *or not*?

I recommend answering these last two questions whenever you feel you are at a crossroads, such as whether to start a project or not, or perhaps to stop working on one. My clients find it extremely clarifying.

Step 4. Embracing Humility

Humility doesn't have very pleasant connotations for most people. To humiliate someone or to be humiliated by someone is not something anyone wants. But on its own, as a noun, it is a very empowering quality. My favorite definition of humility is this: "Humility is not thinking less of yourself. It is thinking *about* yourself *less*."

Journal Prompt A: When and where do you feel self-conscious or self-judgmental? When you are about to show your work? While you are making it? When you reflect on what your hopes are for the work? What are those thoughts? Be as specific as possible.

Journal Prompt B: If you were to take the focus off of yourself and ask "solution-focused" questions pertaining to the matter, what would those be? Hint: Solution-focused questions tend to start with "how," whereas problem-focused questions are either psychoanalytical or not questions at all. For example: "I'll never accomplish this. It's too overwhelming. Why can't I just get on with it? Who do I think I am? [Answer: ambitious, which is good.] I think I'll take a nap." A solution-focused question would be: "How do I begin?"

Finally, it's time to record the answers to your "solution-focused" questions. Be as granular as necessary, even if that's "get up out of bed." Notice if you start judging the answers. If so, know that's you going back to focusing on yourself. Embrace humility by allowing whatever answers want to come to populate the page while dismissing the idea that they're "too pathetic" or "too stupid" (aka unworthy) of you!

 ## In Session and as Homework

I have used this exercise within the context of a group intensive followed by paired sharing, and it would also work well as a homework assignment.

If a client is getting hung up with perfectionistic tendencies about controlling the outcome of the work, it is especially applicable. A conversation about how grandiosity manifests is in order, to check for experiential relevance in the client. It is also important, obviously, that you address any shaming effect the word *grandiosity* may have for them, so that they can own and address the challenge it presents.

 ## For Home Use

Since this is a journaling exercise, all that is needed is a pen, a notebook, and your mind. If you have a coach, therapist, or mentor with whom you can unpack the data afterwards, all the better, but that isn't necessary.

Client Results

This exercise has proven very beneficial to clients of mine who struggle with "compare and despair." A filmmaker who tended to stop herself before she began was finally able to finish her screenplay once she realized it did not require her becoming the next Scorsese. It allowed her to do an end run around the shame she felt at her blockage and objectively analyze it so that she could move on with the work. Personally, I have found it clarifying and invaluable with regard to staying grounded in my own meaning and purpose professionally.

⁎⁎

About Rahti Gorfien

Rahti Gorfien, PCC, is a multi-credentialed career, creativity, and ADHD coach who has been helping artists and entrepreneurs focus so they can grab the focus of others since 2003. Through highly individualized coaching, she gives clients the tools to manage their mind, enabling them to follow through on the strategies co-created during sessions. The result is that they get seen and make money doing what they love. Visit http://creative callingcoaching.com.

This, Not That, More, and Less

35

Anne Ditmeyer

Exercise Purpose

To help creatives find clarity if they are stuck or if they are moving in a new direction.

 Exercise Description

Take a plain piece of paper and fold it in half horizontally and in half again vertically so it forms four equal quadrants. (As an alternative, you can draw two lines on your page to create four squares.)

In the top left square, write "THIS" at the top. (You'll need remaining space in the box to write, so don't make your "THIS" too large, but be sure to have clear headings.)

Continue in the same manner with the other three boxes. The top right-hand box should have a heading that reads "NOT THAT," the bottom left-hand box will read "MORE," and the bottom right-hand box will read "LESS." (It can help to write the headings in all caps, to put a box around them, or to use a different color pen so that they are clearly visible.)

Then in each quadrant, consider:

+ What is a word or phrase that describes what I'm doing (either in life, in my creative life, or with a particular project)?
+ What is a word or phrase that describes what I'm *not* doing? (Or that I don't want to be doing.)
+ What do I want more of in life, in my creative life, in my business, or in this particular creative project?
+ What do I want less of?

Start with whichever box feels right. There are no rules as to how you flow through this document. You'll likely bounce around to the different boxes as new ideas are sparked. You may find there may be set dichotomies (this: self-care, not that: hustle; more: proactive, less: reactive; more: support, less: judgment) as you go through each section, but don't worry about that too much when you get started. Don't edit yourself. Put down anything that comes to mind.

It may help to think in terms of phrases like "This, not that" or "This versus that." You may even want to start in the right-hand column and think, "Less answers, and more questions." If you do find a natural pairing of words, you could add a line to connect the two, or just align them horizontally to form a "match."

When you first do this activity, put down every and any idea in the boxes. Try to get down as much as you can in a single session. Don't write too large, as you'll want enough space to add more ideas. You'll likely end up with many ideas in each quadrant of the grid.

Set a timer for 10 minutes to help ensure you do not overthink things. Then step away and return to it later, either whenever you want to add more words or at a fixed time. Add more words as you see fit. (The beauty of the folded paper is that it's easy to carry with you.)

Try not to erase or cross out anything. Everything on this page may help spark or inspire something later, so don't worry about being the perfect editor. At some point, you may find that you have too many words and ideas on the page. Still, certain ideas will jump off the page and you will feel more pull towards. You can put a star or sticker next to these, or start a new grid that's your "key focus" grid and will serve as your main reminders.

 In Session or as Homework

The creative process can get messy, but we often forget that. In the outside world, we see finished projects and shiny, pretty objects. We rarely see all the work that goes into them. This exercise is designed to have clients reflect on what they actually want and are working towards, and not get distracted by what others are doing or what they think they "should" be doing. We all need reminders of what we're doing and why we're doing it. This one-page grid is something that can generate ideas and that a client can glance at as a quick reminder of what he wants and what he doesn't want.

For Home Use

This exercise is designed to be fun. The simple act of using colored paper and one's favorite pens and markers can bring extra joy to some clients. For others, a ballpoint pen and a plain sheet of paper is all they need.

Some clients may want to make a "messy version" in their notebook or their journal where they dump ideas, but then they may want to make a "clean" version to hang on the wall by their desk to serve as a reminder.

This page can be updated as you go. Consider it a living, breathing document. You may be reading an article or listening to a podcast and hear a word that sparks another idea. Quick, write it down before you forget! We too often forget the obvious.

It's recommended that you start on paper, but it may be something you want to take digital and store somewhere like Google Docs, where you can pull it up wherever you are. The beauty of it being a physical sheet of paper is that it's inspiring to see it hanging next to your desk as a reminder.

If you have some graphic design sensibilities or capabilities, why not make a mini version that you can make into wallpaper for your phone, or print out a small copy to keep in the front of your notebook where you can refer back to it regularly?

 **Client Results**

The first time I suggested this exercise to a client on a call, I didn't know how she would react. Fast forward to the next session and she quoted one of her pairs back to me. "Purpose, not productivity," she said. It was almost as if a giant lightbulb had gone off over her head. The list gave her permission to realize that there were other approaches and narratives than the ones she'd been constantly bombarded by in the business world where she spent so much of her time.

My own list includes "more love and compassion, less judgment" and "more dreaming big, less playing it safe." I know I'm a "cultural observer" but not into "influencer culture." In articulating what I'm not, I find it's forced me to dig into what irks me about a certain thing or a certain context. It allows me to drill down and uncover the aspects of something that do spark excitement in me and the work I do.

We can easily be distracted or thrown off course by someone's comment or by reading about someone else's success. This grid is an excellent visual reminder to always come back to ourselves and to who we are.

**

 **About Anne Ditmeyer**

Anne Ditmeyer is an American designer, creative coach, and consultant based in Paris, France. With a less traditional background in anthropology, graphic design, and global communication, her superpower is connecting the dots. She pulls from her toolbox of creative tools in design thinking and user experience design to approach coaching in a creative way, working with clients one-on-one around the world and through facilitating creative workshops. She believes the power of coaching comes from asking more questions, not trying to have all the answers. You can find more of her work at anneditmeyer.com and on social media at @pretavoyager.

Draw Your Way Forward

36

Rachel Marsden

Exercise Purpose

This exercise is designed to help creatives find new solutions to their current challenges, to break through blocks, and to overcome creative anxieties.

 Exercise Description

Sometimes when we have a challenge we can get stuck trying to "think" our way out. Image-making and the use of metaphor can help us step out of our default way of thinking and open up to new creative solutions.

In Session and as Homework

Step 1. Drawing the Image

Drawing an image can externalize an internal dilemma, creating a distance from it so that it can be experimented with, disrupted, cut out, colored in, reshaped, or erased. The client draws his dilemma using abstract forms, and the coach asks questions to coax out insights using the image as the exploration point.

The client is invited to either change the image in some way or to create a new image that reflects a desired outcome. The coach and client then discuss what actions or internal changes would serve to bring the client to the desired outcome.

This exercise is useful for creative people working in any field. In session, you would ask your client to draw her "challenge" using abstract forms and the devices of abstraction like color, line, shape, and metaphor. Assure her that she doesn't need to have any drawing or painting abilities. She won't be creating a finished "product" for anyone else to look at. Provide her with paper and colored pens, pencils, paints, or crayons. Magazines can also effectively be torn up and glued onto a page to make abstract shapes.

When working with visual artists, encourage them to use materials they normally wouldn't use. Crayons are great to help artists step away from their default art-making mode.

Before your client begins, suggest that she take a few deep inhales and exhales to come into a relaxed state. Or you might like to provide clients with a short relaxation meditation.

Step 2. Asking Process Questions

Once your client has created her image, it's time for the coach to ask questions. The following prompts and questions may prove useful:

+ Ask your client to describe what she sees, as literally as she can, as though she were looking at it for the first time.
+ Ask her about each of the different elements in the drawing and what the elements might mean or suggest to her.
+ Ask her if there were elements in the image that surprise her or that she wasn't expecting.
+ Turn your client's image upside-down and ask her if she can see a solution or an alternative from this vantage point.
+ Ask your client if there are any positive messages she can take from the image or if the image suggests something that needs to be acknowledged.

Be wary of going too wide in the questioning or letting the free association stray too far away from the topic. Some find this questioning process fun and engaging, whereas others find it frustrating and counter-productive. For the latter, keep your questions as closely related as possible to the dilemma the client is exploring.

Do not interpret your client's image. Your client is making a lot of creative connections on her own, and that is the most important part of the process. Avoid making comments about her technical abilities, good as well as bad, as value judgments can block her process. In many cases, the process of simply drawing in a quiet and supportive environment will provide clients with useful epiphanies.

Step 3. Inviting Transformation

Now that your client has created a full picture of her dilemma, it's time to find possible solutions. There are two main ways to do this. Choose the option that makes the most sense to you or invite your client to choose the option that makes the most sense to her.

Option 1. Invite your client to change her current image so that it is "improved." This might mean adding new elements, cutting something out, turning it in a new direction, or drawing over the top of it.

Option 2. Invite your client to create a new image that depicts how she would like things to be. She might use elements from the original image or it might be a completely different drawing. Once she's created the second image, you can ask questions to help her build a bridge from her current state (the first image) to where she wants to be (the second image).

Whether your client adopts option one or two, encourage her to name and choose some actions to take based on what she has learned through the image-making process.

 For Home Use

This exercise can be done without a coach by following these steps. You can employ the sample questions as starting points or you can make up your own. It's important that you write down your answers, as that helps you ground your insights.

 Client Results

This exercise can be used to explore all kinds of creative dilemmas. Perhaps someone is blocked and feels as if she has no ideas. With pen and paper, she can draw an abstract image of what that block looks like. How tall is it? How wide is it? Is it a brick wall or a barbed wire fence? Then a coach might ask, "Visualize how you might get past that block." Might the client employ a ladder, a bridge, some stone steps, or dynamite?

This exercise is especially good for perfectionism or persistent self-doubts. Clients can see the internal "thing" outside of themselves and symbolically alter it. They can experiment with being imperfect. Or they might pin up the image somewhere easily visible so that they could continue to "work on the issue" until they came to some sort of resolution.

One client was feeling anxious about a presentation she had to give the following day. I asked her to draw what that anxiety looked like. It was a scribble of messy, flame-like colors. We explored the image, naming and acknowledging the fears. Then I turned the image upside-down and asked her if she could find a positive message in what she saw.

Her face immediately lit up. "I see a powerful queen with a crown and wings," she said. There were pink elements that represented benevolence. Red represented passion. I invited her to add anything to the image that would make it even more powerful. She strengthened the body section a bit but otherwise left it alone, explaining that it was perfect as it was.

I suggested that she physically embody the queen that she saw. How would the queen sit? Stand? Breathe? I suggested that she imagine herself as the queen whenever she started to have anxious feelings during the presentation. After the presentation was over, she reported that she had felt calm and confident throughout. The image now lives on the wall of her office to permanently remind her of her strength.

 About Rachel Marsden

Rachel Marsden is an Australian artist coach living in Berlin, Germany. She works with creative professionals across the spectrum of the creative industries, helping them thrive, prosper, and find fulfillment. More about her coaching and creative work can be found at www.thegreatcreativelife.com.

A Haiku a Day

Creative Mindfulness to Break Blocks

37

Jennifer Duncan

Exercise Purpose

To transform negative self-talk and over-rumination into creative focus and awareness, enabling greater unimpeded access to the flow state.

 Exercise Description

Among twenty snowy mountains
the only moving thing
was the eye of the blackbird
                    —Buson

Creatives are given the task of writing one haiku every day for a week. This is not the 5-7-5 haiku of grade school language arts. This is haiku as meditation in action, grounded in paying attention to the world and staying open to "the haiku moment," when one is struck with intense awareness of something outside oneself, transcending ego.

The exercise begins with explaining this idea and looking at examples of haiku from Basho, Buzon, and Issa (easily found with a Google search). The guidelines are:

+ Strict syllable counting is not required (6-8-5 would be fine), but the lines should be short/long/short, with lines 1 and 2 or 2 and 3 enjambed (joined together as a complete thought).
+ No "I" or abstractions (love, freedom, depression, etc.) in the haiku.
+ Look out a window or go to a park or garden and pay attention to nature.
+ Don't think about the assignment or about yourself; just keep awareness focused on the outside world, using all your senses.
+ When "the haiku moment" comes, just take it in; don't write right away.
+ When you feel you've fully taken in the moment, write the haiku, spotlighting one concrete image.
+ Do this daily for one week.

Being fully in the moment, focused with all senses on something tangible outside the self, quiets inner talk and analysis. The haiku trains this ability so it can be used to free ourselves from busy-mind and to enter creative flow.

 In Session or as Homework

Ideally, the session introducing this exercise would involve meeting in a park or taking a walk outside, as being fully physical present with the outside world is foundational to the haiku.

A handout with a description of the haiku as meditation in action, strong examples of haiku, and writing instructions should be prepared ahead of time and given to the client for home use.

After the client has an opportunity to share the inner dialogues interfering with their creative flow, the coach can go over the handout and then the haiku practice can begin.

The client finds an inspiring place to sit and take in the world, with notebook and pen handy. The coach can have the client close their eyes and do deep breathing before looking out at the world and pointing to sensory inspiration in the immediate environment: a bee collecting pollen, a leaf falling, an icicle dripping.

If the session has to be indoors, giving creatives images from nature to practice the haiku can help them understand and get comfortable with process. I keep both a scrapbook and a Pinterest board of such images. The exercise is really meant as outdoor work and homework, though, as the authenticity of "the haiku moment" can be compromised in session and with representations instead of immediate experience.

Creatives who are very resistant to writing can instead go to a park and make artist trading card–sized sketches of items from nature: an acorn, an apple. This can still fulfill the intention of focusing on something specific and concrete outside the self and meditatively stilling the busy internal voice.

 For Home Use

After one week of this daily practice, creatives have the option of continuing with haiku as a discipline of mindfulness. The exercise can be extended in many ways as well. An artist journal can be made to collect and illustrate a collection of haiku. The haiku can become part of the practices of "forest bathing" (spending mindful time in the woods) and "earthing" (walking barefoot) that are now proven to decrease anxiety and increase creative and intellectual focus.

Creatives who benefit from a sense of community can join with others to write rengas. A renga is a long poem composed collaboratively as poets take turns adding a haiku (5-7-5 syllables) followed by a non-rhyming couplet (7-7 syllables). For my creative practice, I filled a jar with my haiku written on slips of paper, and I pull one out when I need a mindful pause in my work.

Client Results

This exercise was first developed in a university classroom setting. Once, I took my introductory creative writing class to sit under a circle of willows by a pond to teach haiku, and as I explained "the haiku moment," a rabbit hopped up and sat beside me. There is a kind of magic to it.

Outside of coursework, I give this exercise to any creative writing, theatre, music, or visual art student who is asking for help with blocks rooted in self-talk and over-rumination—and all have reported that it helped break the block and inspire new work. When I run into former students years later, they often exclaim that they embraced this exercise as a lifelong habit, as it continues to help them regain focus in their creative processes.

Recently, I gave this exercise to an academic instructor who was struggling with over-thinking and having difficulty entering creative flow in her artwork. Two of the haiku she produced had particular aesthetic merit (although all were strong):

> Two monarchs whirling
> Above a streetlamp
> Maple leaves falling on light
>
> Ragweed blossoms
> Twelve honeybees
> Floating on yellow

More importantly for our purposes, she reported: "I found that committing to writing haiku was meditative. I opened my notebook on public transit or paused on my walks to be more attentive to the world. Pausing felt good, too. I was reminded that nature is found in the neighbor's garden as well as the cracks of the sidewalk."

**

 ## About Jennifer Duncan

Jennifer Duncan is a teacher, writer, and artist. She is the author of *Sanctuary & Other Stories* and *Frontier Spirit: Brave Women of the Klondike* and has been teaching in York University's Creative Writing Program for fifteen years while working on a novel and a PhD in Language, Culture and Teaching, specializing in creative pedagogies. She is also the co-creator of the innovative visual culture–based curriculum for the Yukon School of Art. Her art practices include mixed media; assemblage; watercolor; needle and wet felting; embroidery; quilting; fabric dyeing; paper, book, and ink-making; pyrography; and altered clothing. Email her atjinx.duncan@sympatico.ca.

Ask Your Muse 38

Lisa Tener

Exercise Purpose

This exercise has two primary purposes, to help creatives bypass their inner critic and get the answers to their creative questions from deep within and to help them break through creative blocks and fully express themselves.

 Exercise Description

Step 1. You may want to come to the exercise with one or two questions about your work (Which book to write? How big to make the sculpture? What themes to explore? Can I really do this?). Write them down.

Step 2. Close your eyes and imagine you are walking along a path in the forest. What do you observe as you walk this path? Use a variety of your senses and note what you see, hear, smell, sense, and feel, or even taste as you walk on this path.

Step 3. You'll come to a clearing and a small building or other structure in that clearing. Perhaps you'll see stairs and a door. Walk those stairs and open the door. Perhaps your muse opens the door for you, or you may find your muse in another room. You know exactly how to find your muse.

Step 4. Once you have found your muse, ask your muse your question and wait for an answer. Your answer may be visual, auditory, a symbol, or a felt sense of something. If it's not clear, ask your muse for clarity.

Step 5. When you finish asking your questions, ask your muse if it has anything else it wants you to know.

Step 6. Thank your muse.

Step 7. Exit back through the door and stairs or however you entered. Return to the clearing and then walk through the forest.

Step 8. Open your eyes.

Step 9. Make notes about what your muse communicated and anything else you'd like to capture of the experience.

You can return to this exercise and your muse any time.

 In Session or as Homework

To prepare a client, first determine the challenges the client faces artistically—mindset challenges, sabotaging habits, and/or questions about where to take their work creatively and what their next steps ought to be.

Your client may need clarity about what a "muse" is. Share your understanding of the muse, perhaps as an archetype of the creative source. A muse may be experienced as something internal or external. Let your client know there is no one right way to experience their muse and that they can begin this exercise with a curiosity to see how it shows up for them.

You may also assure your client that if they find themselves second-guessing whether they are "making this up," it doesn't matter whether they are; they can just flow with it.

Let your client know they may experience their muse visually, or in an auditory way (such as an inner voice) or kinesthetically. The muse may be a wise being, a religious figure, a totem animal, an object, a color of light, a felt sense, or something else. Assure them there is no right or wrong answer.

Come up with a list of questions together, based on the client's challenges, questions, and goals. Then lead the client through steps 1 through 9, asking their questions once they connect with their muse and pausing to give them time to receive an answer. They may wish to share their experience as they go through the forest, but they do not need to. Once they communicate with their muse, it is helpful to share what they are "getting" from their muse.

If additional questions come to you, based on one of their answers, feel free to ask.

If your client seems confused by the muse's answer, invite them to ask the muse to provide more clarity. Encourage two-way communication with the muse.

 For Home Use

To use the exercise at home, start with a list of questions you wish to ask your muse. If you have many questions, you may need to look at your list, which could take you out of the deep state of the exercise. So, you may wish to limit the number of questions to begin with.

You can make an audio recording of yourself reading each step of the exercise so you can listen to it and lead yourself through it. Then play the recording, pausing the recording when you need time to spend more time with the answers.

When the exercise is complete, make notes, or just launch into your creative endeavor.

Client Results

Kenya is an educator and author of three successful nonfiction books for adults. She felt an urge to write fiction for young people but wasn't sure this path could really work for her. After all, she wasn't trained in writing fiction. She decided to ask her muse which project to focus on next. Her muse showed up as a "little old lady" smoking a cigarette, staring at her phone and coughing.

Kenya told her muse that she was tired of giving advice in her books, and her muse told her, "We're all tired." Kenya asked her muse whether she should write fiction for young adults. As their banter seemed to go in circles, she found herself asking permission of her muse. "Who the hell am I to give you permission? I'm just a little old lady sitting in a field, waiting for a WiFi connection."

Instead, her muse turned it around and asked Kenya questions about why she wanted to write this book. Kenya discovered layers upon layers of meaning in the project. Kenya became her muse and then the muse became her grandmother, offering Kenya the chance to explore what truly, deeply mattered to her, namely her family. She got in touch with why she wanted to write fiction for young adults and that place within her that she could tap into for the inspiration for this new work.

After this exercise, Kenya found a coach/editor to help her explore this new project and to help her learn the craft. She continued to access her muse for inspiration and to enjoy this new way of writing, which brought delight, a sense of play, and reinvigorated her creatively.

**

 ## About Lisa Tener

Stevie Award–winning book coach Lisa Tener guides creatives, entrepreneurs, experts, healers, and visionaries to joyfully write their books and publish successfully. Lisa also blogs widely, serves on the faculty of Harvard Medical School's publishing course, and teaches book writing and publishing courses. She enjoys coaching clients to get in touch with their muse and reach new heights of creativity, to write more powerfully, and to write book proposals and books that achieve their goals and bring their vision to life. Many of her clients have received five- and six-figure book deals and have won prestigious awards. Website: Lisatener.com. Email: Lisa@Lisatener.com. Twitter: @LisaTener.

Dance Your Heart Out

39

Steph Cohen

Exercise Purpose

Our creative process is an ever-evolving, living thing. It requires just as much attention, care, and love as we do. Most of us create because we have an unquenchable inner desire. When that desire is muted it can cause stress, anxiety, low mood, fractiousness, and more. This can lead to procrastination, over-complication, discrediting what we've already made, or simply giving up. When a client comes to me with these issues, I help them to navigate their way from creative full stop to accepting the bumps that are a part of their creative process. I help them utilize the difficulty they face as an opportunity to try doing things differently.

 Exercise Description

If you feel like you've been struggling to start, are uninspired, bored with your creative routine, or just want to change things up a bit, this exercise is for you. It's designed to leave you feeling lighter, refreshed, and renewed so that you can create joyfully and freely unencumbered by any mental or physical heaviness.

It's particularly helpful for those who stand and paint for hours on end or sit hunched over, drawing or making objects. Playing with this exercise can help to boost endorphins, release tense muscles, oxygenate your blood, focus your mind in a relaxed way, and leave you feeling more in control of your time and process.

 In Session or as Homework

The exercise is called Dance Your Heart Out. Have you ever seen anyone dancing to a piece of music they really love without them having a smile on their face or wearing some dreamy expression? We've all seen this reaction in children and adults the world over. Music and movement simply create a magical feeling that nothing else can replicate.

What You Need

+ A space of any size. Don't let a small space put you off. A small space can actually challenge you to become even more creative with your movement!
+ Some favorite music, anything that makes you smile and want to move to when you hear it!

Before You Start

It's really important to prepare your body, especially if you've been sedentary for a while. I recommend doing some spinal rolls and gentle swings to wake your body up. Here's how to do them.

Spinal Rolls: With your feet hip distance apart, toes facing forward and a slight bend in your knees, take a breath in. As you exhale slowly, gently allow your chin to drop naturally towards your chest. Allow this motion to continue down each vertebra of your spine as you fold forwards, dropping your shoulders, rolling down towards your chest, stomach, hips, knees, and toes very slowly and gently, exhaling as you go.

Allow the knees to bend as you roll forward. This releases the lower back. Let your arms drop naturally towards the floor. Take a deep inhale and on the exhale, feel your feet root into the earth. Push down through your heels and begin slowly rolling back up, starting with your lower back and rolling through each vertebra until your head is the last thing to come up. Repeat as much as needed until you feel more supple, open, and relaxed. Many of us have stiff backs or areas we can't feel. You don't need to roll up and down perfectly. Just listen to your body and do what feels good for you.

Swings: With your feet planted hip distance apart, toes facing forward and a slight bend in your knees, gently turn your torso and head from side to side (facing the left side of the room and then the right side), allowing your arms to swing naturally with you. Keep breathing naturally with the swings. It's important not to force your body to twist. Start small and allow your body to gradually open up in its own time.

Press Play

When you're ready, press play on your favorite tracks and go! You can move as gently or as fiercely as you wish (making sure to be careful of your back, your knees, or any injuries you may have). Dance with all your heart and soul in whatever way you wish for as long or short a time as you wish. You could imagine you're moving with the gentle currents in the ocean or reliving a fabulous concert you went to years back. There are no rules, only how you want to move in the moment.

Variations

If you have limited movement capability, that needn't stop you from doing this exercise. You can do this sitting and only moving your arms, shoulders, and head. You could also do it lying down and allowing the breath to move through your body, undulating. Remember, your imagination is limitless and can always take you where you need to go. Sometimes dancing in your mind is enough to release you from the tension of the day.

 ## For Home Use

Use these instructions to engage with this exercise at home.

 ## Client Results

Notice how different you feel from start to finish. You may feel like journaling or jotting down a few ideas after you've finished your movement. Freeing up your body often frees up your thinking. My clients love doing this at home, because they literally get to dance like no one's watching.

It's all too easy to feel overwhelmed or heavy with the weight of starting or completing a project and marketing and selling it. This exercise wakes you up and frees you up to help you let go of all that heaviness and embrace the joy of doing the work you love with a lighter heart.

 ## About Steph Cohen

Steph Cohen is an actress, writer, and creativity coach from the UK who is currently based in Spain. She has a degree in English Literature from Cambridge University, a degree in Contemporary Dance from Birkbeck and The Place, and has worked across multiple industries including dance, literary publishing, finance, marketing, graphic design, and more. As well as pursuing her own creative career, Steph coaches artists of all disciplines to help them discover what works for them to create consistently and joyfully while achieving their deepest creative dreams. You can find out more at www.creativebeingcoaching.com or email her at steph@creativebeingcoaching.com.

Creating Bridging Rituals   **40**

Sheryl Garratt

Exercise Purpose

This exercise describes a simple way to shift energies as you move between creating or performing and daily life or as you ease from one type of task to another type of task.

 Exercise Description

Ritual is not a word we often use in the 21st century. We're too busy juggling our different commitments, multi-tasking, building new portfolio careers, and dealing with technology that has us connected and contactable instantly, 24/7. Yet even in our fast-paced and often frantic lives, ritual can be a way of reclaiming space, of bringing us back into the present moment.

And as artists and creatives, we need that sense of space. We need to be fully present, in order to do our best work. Bridging rituals are the tiny things we can do to help us move smoothly from one role to another, to shift from one task to a different one, to change our state of mind and find focus in a world of constant distraction.

You'll have some of these rituals already, without even planning them: your morning coffee, the playlist you put on while writing, the walk you take with your partner or dog every evening to wind down, the stretches you do every night before sleep, or just the act of fluffing your pillows before getting into bed.

Rituals needn't be complicated or time-consuming. Clearing your desk, making a drink, playing specific music, taking a few seconds to appreciate the look and smell of a meal before eating it, hanging up your coat when you get in, and taking a second to really *feel* that you've arrived home and are leaving work behind: these small things can all help enormously, bringing us back into the here and now.

With creative work, a bridging ritual can be as simple as walking into your workspace, taking a breath, and saying to yourself, "I am here to write/design/make art/music. I am fully present and open."

In Session and as Homework

Create Your Own Bridging Ritual

First, think about your daily life and the different roles you take. Lover, parent, artist/maker, administrator, business owner, teacher, student, friend, housekeeper, cook, manager, etc.

Now think of a situation in which you regularly move from one task, energy, or role to another, and where you notice there is sometimes a hangover from the previous activity. Perhaps, after making work, you have a tendency to drift back to your art in your head, and then you fail to really hear your child or your partner telling you about their day.

Or perhaps, as you make your creative work, your domestic to-do list is still running like ticker tape across the screen of your mind, or you're still re-running an annoying conversation from your day job.

Think of a bridging ritual that might move you more easily from one task to the other, something that can firmly anchor you in the present and turn you fully to the task at hand.

There is no right or wrong here. Create something that works for you. What's important is to choose something that is easy and enjoyable. Put what you need in place to do it. A candle will need matches; if you're going to drink water before switching tasks, keep a glass nearby. When I clear my desk, I wipe it down with a few drops of grapefruit oil, so I keep the oil and a cloth in the desk drawer.

Then simply repeat your new ritual, until it becomes an ingrained habit. At first you will need to consciously say to yourself: "I am now moving from administration to creating," or whatever energy shift you are making. But soon just the act of making the tea, clearing your desk, or turning on the music will be enough to help you get into the correct mindset.

One note of caution here: don't go overboard, inventing new rituals for everything. Put one in place and practice it until it becomes automatic and unconscious, before creating another one.

Most performers already have some sort of ritual in place before they go onstage, whether conscious or not. They might have a warm-up routine, a prayer or mantra they repeat, or a lucky talisman they need to touch before leaving the dressing room.

What is often neglected is a wind-down ritual, to use when the performance is over, the autographs are signed, and you are once more alone. Many performers turn to unhealthy stimulants to continue the buzz, the heightened emotions they felt onstage. Instead, it is better to consciously return to the everyday world, to take off the stage persona and let go of the adrenalin rush and the euphoria of performing. This can take the form of cool-down exercises, some conscious breathing or a quick meditation, or anything else that grounds you and brings you back into the rhythms and pleasures of everyday life.

 For Home Use

Using the instructions, create one or more bridging rituals of your own.

 **Client Results**

To help you create your own bridging ritual, here are some more examples from my own practice as a coach working with creatives.

One artist who came to me with procrastination issues chose to play the same song every time she entered her studio to work and then light a scented candle. The candle remained lit while she was working, but she snuffed it out every time she stopped working or thinking about working for longer than a few minutes. Just the act of lighting and relighting it made her more conscious of when she had lost focus. Within a month, music and candle were all she needed to reach her goal of 4 hours of concentrated work per day.

Another artist I worked with had a small studio only a few steps from the back door of his home. Nonetheless, he decided to walk to work, doing ten slow, deliberate, and meditative circuits of his yard clockwise before starting to paint, then ten in the opposite direction to wind down at the end of his day. At first his wife watched incredulously as he slowly passed by their kitchen window again and again, but she soon appreciated that when he finally came through the door, he was fully present and *with* her, rather than still preoccupied with his painting.

A set designer who was used to running big teams realized that she was bringing this energy home, which was causing conflict. At her workshop, she directed skilled artisans, who expected terse commands and tight deadlines, but she was directing her partner and their two small children in much the same way, and toddlers especially don't respond well to such pressure!

We worked on a new bridging ritual for returning home. After parking on her driveway after work, she now plays a favorite aria on the car stereo, closes her eyes, and breathes deeply while letting go of the day. She then enters the house via the garage, showers, and changes out of her work clothes. Then she greets her children as their mother, not their boss.

**

 About Sheryl Garratt

Sheryl Garratt has earned her living as a writer and magazine editor for more than thirty years. For the past decade, she has also worked as a coach supporting creatives of all kinds, helping them to step up and do their best work, in an inspired, juicy, and sustainable way. You can find her at www.thecreativelife.net. Visit the website to download her free ten-day course, Survival Skills for Freelance Creatives.

Alphabet to the Rescue 41

Saundra Alexis Heath

Exercise Purpose

Alphabet to the Rescue consists of three exercises used alone or in combination to help creatives deal with creative anxiety.

 Exercise Description

Exercise 1. Deep Breathing. Clients are instructed to take twenty-six deep Alphabet breaths, one deep breath and exhale for each letter of the alphabet, until they have completed all twenty-six letters. This exercise helps clients calm themselves and focus during breath work.

Exercise 2. Alphabet Parade Visualization. Clients are instructed to visualize each letter of the alphabet written on a page and the twenty-six pages strung together. They are instructed to softly state each letter as they visualize this parade of letters. This exercise can be repeated two times. Clients are asked to describe the alphabet pages. Are the pages plain or colorful? Are they decorated? The coach can lead clients through visually decorating the alphabet page. The coach can also guide clients in increasing or slowing down the pace of the parade of letters.

Exercise 3. Alphabet Affirmations. The coach instructs clients to think of a positive description, each beginning with a different letter of the alphabet, and to recite those words in alphabetical order, following an "I Am" statement. For example, "I am Able, I am Bold, I am Confident, I am Determined, I am Excellent . . ." This exercise is repeated several times using different alphabet descriptors. It is excellent for assisting clients in replacing negative thoughts and also works as well in groups as with individual clients. Clients are allowed to "make up" words for the more difficult letters, "X," "Y," and Z."

These exercises are powerful in their simplicity and connecting clients with something comforting and familiar, the alphabet. For clients who have experienced trauma at school, the Alphabet Parade visualization is not recommended, as a client's visualization could place them back in a childhood classroom.

In Session or as Homework

The deep breathing exercise can be used to help clients become present for the session. For clients who do not enjoy or find their mind wandering during breath work, reciting the Alphabet helps focus their attention. In using this exercise at the start of the session, it is not necessary to use the entire alphabet.

This is a great exercise to instruct clients for at-home use or any time they are experiencing anxiety, i.e., before or after a difficult conversation, before a studio visit, or before a gallery talk or other public appearance.

A variation on this exercise might be to have clients breathe in courage, boldness, confidence, or whatever attribute is empowering along with each letter during the breath work. Or they might breathe in an empowering word that begins with each letter of the alphabet. This adaptation would be similar to Alphabet Affirmations but adding breath work.

Alphabet Parade Visualization can also be adapted to paper as a mindfulness exercise for in-person sessions. The client takes a page of paper and, using the whole page, writes each letter of the alphabet on the page. The page should be filled with twenty-six letters. The client should be instructed to write the alphabet in a row with four to six letters in a row. The letters must be handwritten using pencil, pen, marker, or paint. Once the letters have been written, the client is instructed to go over the letters in the same or different format at least five more times.

Alphabet Affirmations can be a really fun exercise that gets clients to bring out their inner courage and shift from negative, victimized thinking. The coach should encourage clients to recite their "I Am" affirmations as though they were bragging to their Momma, a best friend, or reciting the affirmations as a rock star on a concert stage. They could also recite the I Am Alphabet Affirmations as a critical review of their work. For example, they might say, "According to reviewer Jane, I Am Amazing, My work is Best in Show, I am Collector Worthy, Definitely Worth Watching . . ." and so on.

For Home Use

The three exercises form the basis of a creative anxiety management toolkit and should be presented to clients as something that can be used at home at any time, daily, as part of a mindfulness practice, and/or as needed.

The exercises can be used separately or in combination with one another. Deep Breathing can be used upon waking. Alphabet Parade can be used as a creative journaling exercise, and the Alphabet Affirmations can be used before a creative communicates with the outside world, virtually or in person.

An at-home variation for Alphabet Parade Mindful Creative Journaling is to have the client use a different page for each letter of the alphabet and one letter per day. Clients can decorate the page, journal on the page, and add the page to other journals. The idea is to use creating an alphabet-a-day page as a way to reduce stress and anxiety by mindfully creating. It is critically important that the emphasis be placed on the process of creating and not the outcome. Attachment to the Alphabets "turning out" a certain way will negate the mindfulness aspect of the exercise.

Client Results

All three exercises have been used with different clients, alone and in combination. They have the individual and collective effect of creating calm and increasing inner peace and confidence.

In working with an actor who suffered from anxiety around remembering lines and having difficult conversations, Alphabet Breathing helped take the wind out of anxiety attacks and got her to calm down. Alphabet Affirmations minimized or eliminated the often-ensuing negative self-talk and helped her get back on track. When she began feeling stressed, she would quickly doodle an Alphabet Parade on any available sheet of paper. This client reported that it was very helpful to have these tools to prevent or minimize negative emotions or negative thoughts from escalating.

I have used the Alphabet Parade as a morning mindfulness creative journaling exercise in my own work. This involves creating a page of alphabets in pencil and then going over the alphabets in marker or watercolor paint. This exercise at the start of the morning creates an inner joyfulness and is a gift of creativity to myself each day.

The exercise I have used most frequently is Alphabet Affirmations. I have used this frequently in both individual and group sessions. It is particularly useful when a client is struggling with negative self-talk and a negative self-image. The Alphabet Affirmation guides clients in reframing negativity into something positive and empowering. This exercise has an almost immediate effect in shifting a client's energy and perspective.

One client in particular who was reeling from hurtful and negative industry gossip used this exercise to recover her self-esteem. Every time a wave of negative thoughts about herself or anyone else would cross her mind and she could feel the welling up of anxiety, she would begin to recite Alphabet Affirmations to herself.

In a group setting, I have used this exercise at strategic points in a training to unify the group and reduce the anxiety of the unknown and being present with strangers. In a circle, each person creates and recites one affirmation using the alphabet until twenty-six affirmations have been spoken and/or everyone has had the chance to create and recite an Alphabet Affirmation.

At first, there may be some awkwardness and vulnerability about this public recitation. However, as each person takes their turn reciting, it creates a shared experience, and the group will experience a lessening of anxiety and a sense of being accepted and affirmed by the group.

**

About Saundra Alexis Heath

Saundra Alexis Heath is the co-founder and director of Heath Gallery New York, a boutique, contemporary art gallery located in a townhouse in Central Harlem's historic district. She brings to this role more than thirty years' experience in corporate marketing and brand-building. Heath Gallery New York's signature event, HangNight™, provides easy-access exhibition and performance opportunities for early-career artists. As a brand strategist and creativity coach, Saundra teaches an online course, "From Ordinary to Extraordinary," that guides creative entrepreneurs in developing the mindset and effective action plans to achieve their personal and professional goals. Saundra can be reached at info@saundraheath.com.

Imagine, Create, Transform 42

Steevie Jane Parks

Exercise Purpose

This is a very flexible expressive arts exercise that helps people to successfully integrate conflictual feelings, as well as conflictual "identity states." It typically involves the use of an easily moldable substance such as clay, Sculpey, or Model Magic. It can be practiced either alone or in the presence of a trained clinician or a creativity coach. My rule of thumb is that if you are planning to share this exercise with clients who have significant psychological issues, you need to have a clinician present.

 Exercise Description

I generally recommend giving the client a choice of materials to use that fit in with their level of comfort with making messes and their experience with sculpting in general. Since I originally developed this exercise as a therapy tool, I have always strongly encouraged people to focus on process over outcome. The goal is not to create a sculpture that looks good, but to create a meaningful reminder of what the client has learned in the process of creating it.

Over the past thirty-plus years, I have witnessed many a dramatic breakthrough with the use of this relatively straightforward technique that I developed by working with young children in the 1970s and 1980s. The concepts underlying this technique came from the writings of a variety of well-known art therapists, including Margaret Naumberg and Arthur Robbins.

I highly recommend having quiet instrumental music playing in the background as your client engages in their process. It really helps people to focus on their emotional experience and allows them to enter into their own personal creative trance.

The entire procedure generally takes anywhere from 30 to 60 minutes, depending on how deeply engaged your client becomes in the task. If you are presenting the experience to a group, it can take up to 3 hours to get around to including everyone in the discussion following completion of the exercise. I have often done this exercise with groups of more than thirty people, and it can take quite a while to process when everyone feels like sharing their experiences.

✺ In Session or as Homework

You'll need:

1. A quiet place to work
2. A work table with a protective surface
3. Instrumental music via a radio, computer, smartphone, or phonograph
4. Some form of easily moldable clay (Sculpey, Model Magic, modeling clay, or even Play-Doh!)
5. A camera to take photos of each step in the process

The exercise can be done with adults, adolescents, elderly people, people over the age of 8 who have the use of their hands, and anyone who enjoys allowing their unconscious minds to symbolically solve real-life problems (e.g., artists/creatives).

Step 1. Have the person get comfortable in their chair and explain to the person that they are going to be creating things with clay with their eyes closed while listening to music.

Step 2. Separate a large piece of modeling material into two equal-sized balls. Each ball should be about the size of a large scoop of ice cream. Place the two balls in front of the subject/client/yourself.

Step 3. If you are skilled in the use of hypnosis, you can induce a mild trance by having your client (or yourself, if you are doing this alone) close their eyes and focus on their breathing. You can instruct the subject to breathe in creative energy and to breathe out fear, apprehension, or anxiety.

Step 4. Instruct the subject to close their eyes and to think about something that is presenting a problem for them in their current life. This can be either a negative aspect of themselves, another person, a negative situation in their environment, or even a negative destructive feeling that they would like to get rid of. Turn on some quiet, peaceful instrumental music as you instruct the client to pick up the first ball of clay.

Step 5. Instruct the client to think about the negative feelings that they associate with the "problem" that they wish to solve, while allowing their hands to create either a symbol or a realistic object that represents the problem. Tell them to keep forming the ball of clay in their hands with their eyes closed until the shape feels completed. Then have them open their eyes as they set this piece of work aside.

Step 6. Important: Take a photo of object number one when it is completed.

Step 7. Take a short break.

Step 8. Put on the music again and repeat having your client close their eyes after picking up the second of the two balls of modeling material. This time have your client think about a positive quality or a positive situation that they would like to manifest, either in their personal lives or in the outside world in general. Have them sculpt this quality or situation either as a symbol or an actual representational object with their eyes closed while listening to the same music. When they feel satisfied with the way the sculpted object feels in their hands, have them open their eyes and put it down.

Step 9. Again, take a photo of object number two and take another short break.

Step 10. Now it's time for the exciting part of the exercise, the part that enables the symbolic integration to occur. Have your client start listening to the same music with their eyes closed, but this time instruct them to pick up their two sculptures and to allow the music as well as their "wise mind" or "unconscious mind" to guide their hands as they find a unique way to combine both objects into one large object. Let them know that this process must be done intuitively with their eyes closed, and that what they end up sculpting will be unique and will represent an answer to the problem that they have been struggling with.

This part of the exercise can take a fairly long time. Be aware that for some clients this can be a highly emotional experience. This is why I personally recommend that you have subjects with any type of mental health issue do this exercise in the presence of a trained mental health professional. I have always been present with my clients when I teach them this technique as virtually all of my psychotherapy clients had some type of mental health issue, or they would not have come to see me in the first place.

Instruct the client not to think about the outcome and not to have any preconceived ideas about how the two objects should fit together as one. Let them work on this step as long as they want to. When the new object feels right in their hands, have them open their eyes to see what they have created.

Step 11. Take a photo of object number three.

Step 12. Allow the client to look at all three photos and to fully process the experience before giving them an opportunity to verbalize what the exercise meant to them and what was represented as the symbolic solution to their stated problem.

For Home Use

As mentioned previously, this can certainly be done on one's own. But if there's a reasonable likelihood of a strong emotional reaction, doing it with a trained professional might be a better idea.

Client Results

For clients who have created an object which might inspire them to take positive action steps in their lives, I strongly recommend making the final sculpture as permanent as possible and placing it in a familiar location in their home or office or studio, where they can glance at it often. In this way, they will have a constant reminder that helps them continue to affirm their desire to achieve their goals.

Coaches will be truly amazed at the kinds of symbolic solutions their clients will arrive at by using this kind of creativity coaching exercise. The basic steps can be adapted to fit almost any type of issue that your creativity clients might be struggling with. I have done this exercise in large groups of non-therapy clients and have always been extremely gratified by the results.

I always modify the instructions to fit the people and groups that I work with. For example, the most recent group that I used this exercise with were part of a Unitarian Universalist Church. I focused the exercise on helping these people to integrate their concepts of what the world was lacking with what gifts they had inside each of them that might be of value to others.

This format is especially useful in helping people to emerge from creative dry spells. You can encourage your clients to use the feeling of being creatively blocked as the negative emotional state and to use their freely flowing creative energy as the positive quality they want to embody. I tried this with a group of my painting buddies with good and lasting positive results for all!

 ## About Steevie Jane Parks

Steevie Jane Parks, PhD, is a licensed psychologist, a certified creativity coach, as well as a visual artist. She is currently working on a book entitled *Healing Through Creative Self Expression: Stories of Artists Who Have Healed Themselves Through Their Art*. Steevie has been in practice as a clinical psychologist for more than thirty years and is currently only accepting new creativity coaching clients over the phone. She can be reached at drsjparks@gmail.com.

These are her current working websites:
www.drsjparks.com
www.steevijane.gallery

Don't Be Alone With Your Inner Critic

43

Karen Andrews

Exercise Purpose

This exercise can be a continuing practice for the client who is typically resistant because of harsh inner critic energies.

 Exercise Description

This is a three-part practice, to be done right in the studio, at the writing table, or wherever clients do their creative work. Its purposes are: (1) to plan the work session before starting, (2) to externalize and clearly hear the inner critic's litany, and (3) to acknowledge any work completed and a successful session (especially that they showed up at all).

Internal criticizing energies can be invisible, tricky to separate from, and extremely destructive. Without getting a handle on them, these voices, physical sensations, and distorted thoughts can drain all the joy and energy out of one's creative efforts and make the process too unpleasant to want to continue.

I've witnessed that as an artist gets more deeply into their work, the critics get even louder and harsher. I believe they are inner "protectors" who came into being to keep the client safe from family criticism, rejection, getting too visible, or other ancient dynamics.

+ By externalizing the voices onto paper, the client can see and hear overtly what this part is saying.
+ By writing down immediate plans for the session, it makes it less personal, almost like an assignment: it's tangible, it's specific, and it clarifies the purpose.
+ By recording what happened objectively afterwards, it takes some of the wind out of the critic because it shows all the parts of the person that work is getting accomplished.
+ By timing it, the client begins to get through the block by just doing a small, non-threatening amount of work.

Over time the consistency of this will build into a habit. The critic learns that this work really isn't dangerous, and they (the critic) can relax a little.

✿✿ In Session or as Homework

A client engaging with this exercise will need three pieces of writing paper, a pen, and a timer.

Instructions to the client: When you go into your studio, bring in three pieces of paper, a pen, and a timer. This is so that you're not all alone with your critic and so you have a defined amount of time to work and a clear purpose for the session. You can also learn more about what your critic is actually saying to you.

Try doing this every day that you go into your studio for a few weeks. I may add that I don't believe it's effective to speak disrespectfully of or to our inner critics. They do not like to be demeaned, they are very sensitive to criticism themselves, and they cannot be "gotten rid of." They are important although difficult parts of our psyche, and they need to be handled in particular ways. They carry important concerns for our well-being, they work very hard, and they are very loyal.

Step 1. Client enters studio, and before doing anything else, takes out the three blank sheets of paper and puts a title on each sheet: (1) My Plan for Today's Session; (2) What My Inner Critic Says; (3) What I Accomplished Today.

Step 2. Client sets the timer for 20 minutes. (Client can do less or more, but I personally like 20-minute increments.)

Step 3. Client writes his or her plan for the session: "I will make three studies of the still life, one negative space line exercise, one in charcoal with values, and one thumbnail composition study." Client keeps the page handy in case he or she loses focus.

Step 4. As they begin working, they may start to feel some familiar old feelings arise that usually stop them or make them feel inadequate or want to give up. They stop drawing, listen inside, and write down whatever they just heard their critic say: "You're such a lousy artist; you probably shouldn't even bother doing this; why are you wasting your time?"

Step 5. After jotting it down, they resume their drawing until they hear another such message and repeat the process.

Step 6. At the end of the session when the bell rings, the client stops their work and takes a minute or two to list any and all successes: "Showed up in studio, left the dishes in the sink, washed out my brushes, lined up my paints, filled the water bucket, took a breath, made the first drawing, kept breathing throughout even though I felt tense, made the second drawing, adjusted the lighting, etc." Even the smallest accomplishments count. This recording has multiple purposes, including showing the client's system that "scary" work can get done without setting off any alarms.

I recommend that the client simply collect the pages in a folder. They can bring them in to the coaching session, where we can celebrate the accomplishments and their consistency, and work with some of the specific critic comments. We can work to integrate their parts: their innocent, loving, creative child parts with their ambitious adult parts; their rebellious parts with their frightened parts; etc. In the process, we can both learn more about what needs these criticizing parts are trying to meet.

 For Home Use

This exercise is designed to be done right at an artist's workspace, so it is very well suited for home use.

 Client Results

With some clients, these critics can be relentless at first, and their sessions can involve about 80% critical mutterings. Over time, as they get the critic messages out of their head and onto paper, these mutterings diminish in frequency and power.

Part of our coaching work together is getting to know these parts and dialoguing with them to discover their original reason for doing what they do, and to help them see other ways to accomplish the same goals: real protection, real productivity, etc.

**

 About Karen Andrews

Karen Andrews has intensively practiced many forms of self-help and healing work over the past twenty years as both client and counselor: Co-counseling, Nonviolent Communication (NVC), Community Mediation, Heartmath, Focusing, and Internal Family Systems. She is currently completing her certification for the Creativity Coaching Association. She brings all of these processes and mindsets to her coaching work and enjoys helping creative people unravel their distress and align their parts into a productive, joyful, self-supporting system.

She has worked to integrate and tame her own inner critics and has honed many such techniques to help others do the same. She has been a visual artist for more than thirty years—watercolor, photography, and drawing—and runs a home-based gallery in West Stockbridge, Massachusetts: www.InnerVision-Studio.com. Her coaching website is www.karenandrewscoaching.com. She can be reached through either website or at karenandrewscoaching@gmail.com.

N.A.I.L. Freedom

44

Aneesah Wilhelmstätter

Exercise Purpose

This self-inquiry tool helps creatives take responsibility for the freedom they possess to align their thoughts, attitudes, and behavior with their creative intentions. It helps bring awareness and attention to intention!

 Exercise Description

N.A.I.L. Freedom is a dynamic self-regulation tool crafted to help creatives step into the space between stimulus and response, a space where they have enough freedom to do the next right thing. This four-step alignment process is also an invaluable self-care tool, as it makes room to process accompanying feelings, for instance, by releasing difficult feelings and enhancing positive ones.

In Session or as Homework

The coach can read the following script out loud or clients can read and/or record it for themselves, to be played back and paused as needed. Clients ask and answer the questions, following through by writing down any ideas, impressions, and insights that arise. A client will need 15 minutes, pen and paper, and a willingness to wonder: "What if it were possible for me to get to my creative work no matter what?"

The N.A.I.L. Freedom self-inquiry is made of four elements: **N** for notice and name, **A** for accept and acknowledge (never acquiesce), **I** for inquire with curiosity and compassion, and **L** for let go to live in liberty!

Round One of N.A.I.L. Freedom will help you set in place a pledge to your primary and core intention, which is to practice your creative craft and become the unique individual you need to become in order to practice that creative craft.

I like to call this core intention "yes." Supporting thoughts and actions are the ways you say "yes" to your "yes." Getting to "yes" with yourself begins with figuring out "where you must get to" and in that figuring-it-out process, you are already starting to create the thoughts and actions that will get you there. So let's initiate this "figuring it out" through some pledge-setting.

Begin with noticing: **notice and name** whatever comes up when you think of committing to your creative craft. Without judgment, **accept and acknowledge** the thoughts and feelings that arise. Now, **inquiring** with curiosity, ask and write down the answers to the following three questions:

+ "What work in the service of my creativity do I want to do?"
+ "Am I willing to say 'yes' to doing this work, no matter what?"
+ "Am I willing to say 'yes' to letting go of the grievances that are getting in the way?"

For the fourth step, called "let go to live in liberty!", ask and answer the question, "Am I willing to say 'yes' to living in liberty?"

You might find it beneficial to introduce a sense of ritual and ceremony to this process, for example, by imagining yourself ringing a liberty bell three times while repeating: "Yes, yes, and yes."

Now that your intentions are taking shape, you may be aware of sensations of "yes" and of interfering thoughts and feelings. Round Two is designed to disarm the thoughts and attitudes that might take you out of alignment with your intentions.

To enter into the spaciousness that is present, take a deep breath for a count of five and exhale fully for a count of five. **Notice** the thoughts and feelings that arise; simply witness and name them using the prompts: "I am noticing that I am *thinking* . . ." and "I am noticing that I am *feeling* . . ." **Accept** what is transpiring without acquiescing to devaluations. Next, **inquire** with curiosity and compassion: "What do I need to **let go of**, to get to where I want to go?"

Let your intuition help you name any grievance that may be disturbing you. Write it out on a separate piece of paper and tear it up and discard it while noticing a feeling of release and relaxation. Lastly, practice "**let go to live in liberty!**" by answering the question: "Am I willing to say 'yes' to living in liberty?" You might visualize yourself ringing a liberty bell. To close this round, write and then fold a thank-you note to yourself, beginning it with: "I want to thank me for . . ."

I love Round Three! As you unfold and read your thank-you note, **notice** how it feels when you feel gratitude towards yourself. **Acknowledge** this experience and **inquire**: "Am I willing to say 'yes' to staying with this experience of gratitude for 5 seconds?" Be present with your "yes." Then "**let go to live in liberty!**" and, as you imagine ringing a liberty bell, ask and answer: "Am I willing to say 'yes' to living in liberty?" Complete the practice with a reflection and report on your experiences.

As an alternative approach, you might adapt the exercise by doing one round per night over three nights, gathering additional insights when you wake up each morning by journaling first thing. You might also use any of these questions as a mantra. While any of them can serve that purpose, particularly powerful is: "What if it were possible for me to get to my creative work no matter what?"

 ## For Home Use

As indicated earlier, clients can record their own scripts and play them back, making this an exercise that's ideally suited for home use.

 **Client Results**

Robert, a visual artist, loved being part of a multidisciplinary team at a meditation center, where several times annually, he got to run workshops similar to his own, highly popular offerings back home. He needed to stop his performance-undermining habit of social comparison that caused his stress levels to "shoot to the sky," in spite of the workshop's serene surroundings.

Robert explained: "N.A.I.L. Freedom helped me hold my own 'good enough-ness' by reminding me to stop, take stock, and then step into my authentic story by affirming: 'I am bringing my uniqueness.' Reminding myself what I value about my uniqueness, what it says about me, and then honoring my uniqueness with gratitude helps me show up and shine, instead of doubting my qualifications and value."

As a writer, I know the importance of staying connected to the flow of life I write about. This powerful tool makes it possible for me to regularly write in public by getting my head and heart in the game, no matter what is going on in the crucible of reality. It helps me give myself the thumbs up even when it's noisy, prompting me to play with my perception and let noisiness become an ambient soundtrack.

An attitude of appreciation and gratitude opens my heart to create an inner space of well-being. It helps me tune into my inner wisdom so that I am more receptive to insights, allowing them to come through. It helps me lighten up my thinking so that I can think more clearly and focus more sharply, while bringing a smile to my face and a flow to my pen.

 About Aneesah Wilhelmstätter

Aneesah Wilhelmstätter is a self-taught artist, creativity and life purpose coach, writer, and workshop facilitator. Her life as an expat in the Netherlands, Paris, and London sparked a passion for creative change and transforming herself through her own Hero's Journey. Creator of the Tarot of Experience and author of several books, including *Passion to Performance*, *The Expat's Way*, and *The Thankful Way Journal*, Aneesah worked in the fields of mental health and as a clinical social worker before founding Creative Change Coaching in 2001. Visit Aneesah at:

https://creativechangecoaching.wordpress.com/
and learn about her miracle rituals and ceremonies at
https://miracleroutines.home.blog/

Flip It!

45

Angela Terris

Exercise Purpose

This exercise presents a playful way to bring awareness to internal self-talk. Left unchecked, unhelpful self-talk can bring creative self-doubt, self-criticism, performance anxiety, and procrastination. This step-by-step guide uses a simple process to raise awareness of the impact of unhelpful self-talk on artistic practice.

 ## Exercise Description

This exercise retrains the mind to automatically flip the negative self-talk and replace it with more confident language. It combines wordplay and images, asks four thought-provoking questions, and results in visualizing the new productive self-talk to help you create effortlessly.

In Session and as Homework

The materials you will need are a notebook, a black pen, an index card, and colored pens.

Step 1. To start, let's raise your awareness of the internal mind chatter that you may not be aware is occurring while you create. To do this, have your notebook next to where you work and write down the automatic thoughts that pop into your mind, especially when you feel anxious, frustrated, or stuck. These thoughts highlight when your automatic self-talk has become negative and unhelpful.

You may want to do this over several creative sessions to get a good idea of what you regularly say to yourself. For example, maybe you repeat, "It's not good enough," "I should give up," "I can't do this," or "Who's going to want it?" Begin to notice what you say.

Step 2. Have a look through your notes and choose one word or sentence you would like to get rid of. We will call this your "old limiting belief." You might choose the one that you default to the most. To help you change that negative self-talk, here are four thought-provoking questions to help flip your perspective in the direction of hope:

1. If I was optimistic, how would this limiting belief change?
2. If I was sure that I could not fail, how would I do things differently?
3. If a friend talked to me about this same limiting belief, what would I say to encourage and show understanding?
4. How would I feel and act if I didn't have that thought at all?

Step 3. Reflect on what you've written in response to these four questions and start to bring together your new optimistic belief. It helps to keep it short and memorable, written in the present tense. Make it personal to you and positive. Let's call it your "new confident statement." To make it more effective, choose a symbol that represents your old limiting belief and a symbol that represents your new confident statement.

Step 4. Next, you will need your index card in landscape view. On one side, write down and draw your symbol for the old limiting belief with a black pen. Make the words and symbol small and bland-looking. Flip the card over vertically and use your colored pens to write your new confident statement with its corresponding symbol. Make it bold and appealing.

Practice flipping the card back and forth, lingering on the colored side longer. To make it more powerful, also visualize doing this in your mind's eye. You are now training your brain to reframe your thoughts automatically. The idea is that when negative self-talk pops into your consciousness, you naturally visualize your new vibrant, confident statement replacing it. This will boost your positive feelings and help you decide on the best course of action.

Step 5. You may want to have your new confident statement by your side when working to remind you of your new habit of thinking. And, if you wish, you might go back and repeat this exercise with the other limiting beliefs that you noted earlier.

 ## For Home Use

This exercise is easy to make use of at home, either adapted to your specific needs or used as is.

 ## Client Results

I created this exercise for my coaching client Annie. She was a landscape artist who felt like an imposter and who continuously put her artwork down. During our first coaching call, I became aware that Annie was automatically discounting any successes she had achieved, especially downplaying her skills as an artist.

At the end of the call, I reflected this to her. Annie was surprised. She had not noticed she was doing it or how often it was occurring. I suggested the idea of writing down her self-talk as she worked so she could become aware of it herself and in a few days to email her findings to me.

What became apparent in Annie's email was that her internal self-talk revolved around similar themes: "it's not good enough," "I might fail," "it needs to be perfect," etc. I mentioned this to Annie, and she selected the limiting belief she most wanted to change. Alongside this, I sent the instructions for the Flip It! exercise as a playful way for her to create her new empowering statements and to learn them.

The limiting belief she chose to work on was "It's not good enough." Here are her answers to the four hope-filled questions:

+ If I had more optimism than before, I would believe I was good enough.
+ If I could not fail, I would feel more courageous in my art-making.
+ I would say to a friend, aim for 95% good enough and see what happens. Would anyone else even notice?
+ If I didn't have that thought, I would create without judgment and be more playful and curious.

On one side of her flip card, she wrote the words "not good enough" along with the symbol of a wastepaper bin. On the reverse side, she wrote the words "I create calmly with joy and freedom," and chose the symbol of a shooting star.

When Annie felt the old frustrations creeping in, she consciously checked in with her self-talk and looked at her card and her symbol to remind her to flip to the new confident language. Eventually, it became a new habit to check in with her mind chatter and ensure that her internal dialogue was supporting her in her progress.

The outcome for Annie was that she compared herself less to others and became more focused on her creative path. She relaxed more into the creative flow and reignited her passion for her art-making.

 About Angela Terris

Angela Terris is an artist, book author/illustrator, and creativity coach with a background in creative business, non-profit art organizations, and psychology. She now draws on her experience and knowledge to coach creatives to be bolder and braver in their artistic choices. She works mainly with individuals and creative businesses to develop calm, clear confidence in fulfilling their creative potential. Angela trained at Chelsea School of Art in London and set up her first creative business at the age of 22. She is best known for her book illustration, uplifting paintings, and passion for supporting creatives.

Website: www.angelaterris.com
Instagram: @angelaterris

Symbolic Visualization for Creatives

46

Marj Penley

Exercise Purpose

Symbolic visualization benefits creative folks in numerous and powerful ways. For example, symbolic visualization enables us to become aware of the obvious and obscure aspects of ourselves and to incorporate them not only into our conscious awareness but also into our creative work. Symbolic visualization often results in deeper, richer, and more significant creative work.

 Exercise Description

We will want to begin the exercise by relaxing in a comfortable position, closing our eyes, and choosing a particular symbol for our focus.

We can choose from any of the following symbols: nature symbols, animal symbols, human-made symbols, or religious and mythological symbols. We can also choose from all the symbols that lead to transpersonal experiences: symbols of ascent, expansion, light, fire, development, liberation, and growth.

For this exercise, let's focus on symbols of ascent and light. First, put yourself in a relaxed, comfortable position and close your eyes. Then imagine yourself in a meadow on a pleasant summer day. You might notice some blue jays nearby or some redwing black-birds balanced on sturdy weeds.

You see a path to your right, leading up a mountain. As you walk up this path, you see many rocks on either side. Occasionally, you see some white or purple wild flowers growing between the rocks. As you climb higher and higher, you see just bare rocks. After awhile you reach the top of the mountain and you find a comfortable place to sit.

For the past several weeks you have been bothered by a particular problem. You allow yourself to focus on that problem. With the sunlight shining down on you, you feel not only warm but you also sense how the light is helping you to see more clearly a solution to the problem. You stay on top of the mountain, enjoying the warmth, the light, and a feeling of relief now that you know the solution to your problem.

In Session or as Homework

Symbolic visualization can be used in session or given as homework to develop latent qualities and skills. Whether in session or at home, the person first gets into a comfortable, relaxed position and closes his eyes. For this symbolic visualization, let's focus on growth and development.

First, we ask the person to focus on a particular plant. This plant represents any qualities or skills that the person wants to develop. The person first visualizes tilling the soil, then planting the seed, visualizing the sun and rain falling on the ground, the seed maturing into a young plant, and the young plant then maturing into a full-grown plant.

Since the development of the plant represents the growth of the qualities or skills, as the plant develops, the qualities and skills will develop as well. The client can then imagine a seed of a different plant, representing a different desired quality or skill. He imagines that plant now growing into a fully developed plant and, with the visualization of that plant growing, he imagines the development of that second desired quality or skill as well.

 For Home Use

Creatives can easily adapt this technique of symbolic visualization for home use. A creative person can choose a symbol to represent the current piece of creative work. As he runs into problems or difficulties with the creative work, he can imagine the symbol changing in such a way that the problem or difficulty would be corrected.

For example, a crooked piece of rope might symbolize that there was a problem with the plot of a novel. As the fiction writer imagined straightening out the rope, he would begin to see how to straighten out his novel's plot problems.

Client Results

Whenever Mike was frustrated with his artwork, he took out his anger on his wife. He would yell at her, telling her that she ruined his concentration and that she was destroying his career as an artist. Yet he said that he knew she was not really the cause of his frustration.

He said, "When I feel frustrated with my art, I just see red and I start yelling and blaming my wife." I asked him to think of something that was red. He immediately said, "A rose. A red rose comes to mind."

I suggested to him that he lean back, relax, and close his eyes. I asked him to imagine that he was looking at a red rose. When I asked him what he saw, he said, "Oh, yes, I see the red rose. In fact, I see a whole bunch of red roses. A dozen red roses just like I gave my wife on Valentine's Day."

"It sounds like you love your wife. Is that true?" I asked.

"Oh, I do love her. It's just that I get so damn frustrated."

"I wonder, Mike, if you would be willing to try an experiment?'

"Sure, if it will help."

"The very next time you begin to feel angry, I want you to find a comfortable place, sit down, close your eyes, and imagine a red rose or a bunch of red roses—like those you gave your wife on Valentine's Day. Focus on the red roses."

When Mike came a week later, he could hardly wait to tell me about his experience.

"When I felt frustrated with my art project, I did that thing you suggested. I immediately lay down on the couch and imagined a dozen red roses. I just kept breathing and imagining red roses. In no time at all, my anger melted away. I'm going to do that rose thing every time I start to feel frustrated with my art. I think I'll buy my wife a dozen red roses as well. Just to let her know I really do love her."

 About Marj Penley

Marj Penley's work is all about growth and expansion. For more than thirty years, she has worked with clients who have overcome limitations and expanded their abilities. Marj is a certified hypnotherapist, licensed therapist, and certified creativity coach. She also designs, creates, and sells her own ceramics, paints with watercolors, writes, and has published works on Collingwood's Theory of Art. She will soon have a book published on creativity. With techniques galore, Marj loves to support, guide, inspire, and empower people worldwide.

Marj welcomes email at marjpenley@gmail.com. More about her coaching, classes, and workshops can be found at her website, www.marjpenley.com.

Fused Creative Blocks

47

Midori Evans

Exercise Purpose

Fused Creative Blocks helps creatives create a clear and visual path for action.

 ## Exercise Description

First get a set of index cards. You might want to choose a multi-colored pack so that you have some choices that mirror your thoughts and your moods. Carve out about 20 minutes on a day when you think you have some perspective on the issue you've been struggling with lately. Then find a place that limits distractions.

Spend the first few minutes reconnecting with yourself. Then try to name the feelings or thoughts you want to shed. The naming could be as simple as picking one word that describes an emotion or it might be a phrase that tends to jump into your thoughts and stops you from creating. Write each emotion or thought pattern on a separate index card.

When you are finished with that, continue as follows. Pick some new index cards to use to describe how amazing it feels to connect to your work, to produce something, or to spend time with what you love. If possible, try to have this pile be the same size as the first pile.

After completing both piles, find a place for your index cards to live. Some people pin them up on a poster board near their desk or put them up in the kitchen, creating a display of those two juxtaposed states: the chaos we fall into, on the one hand, and how good we feel when we are creating regularly, on the other hand. This then becomes a visual prompt that helps get you out of your circling thoughts, forcing you to look at how you could be feeling. Grab one of those affirming cards now, hold onto it, and enjoy the physicality of that feeling in your hand.

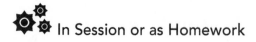 ## In Session or as Homework

Setting up for this exercise is easy. Supplies are merely index cards and a set of colored pencils. Explain to your client that the emotions, possibilities, and limitations we all live with are all fair game to explore in this exercise.

The coach and the client can prepare by spending a few minutes talking about how we all sometimes get stuck in rigid thinking. By naming our limiting thoughts, we open doors. There are no *right* answers in this exercise and no *perfect* set of cards. This is an individualized exercise that will highlight a path forward that is different for each person.

This exercise works well when done in session because the client has something concrete at the end to put up at home or at work. It is so easy to come up with excuses when we are alone or in our own routine. Having the support of a coach and these visual reminders help us stay focused and avoid resistance and blockage.

Once the exercise is completed in session, a client will be familiar with the process and can go deeper the next time around, whether it's during coaching or on their own at home.

 ## For Home Use

Fused Creative Blocks is an easy, self-guided exercise designed for anyone experiencing a creative block. It is easy to adapt and can be used with whatever materials you have on hand. Some people prefer sticky notes to index cards.

When I want to assign this exercise for homework, I first check in with my clients to find out if they prefer the hands-on paper approach or a digital approach. Some already have access to digitally-based sticky notes; for those who want to explore, stormboard. com is one option for using this exercise in a digital format.

 ## Client Results

I have used this exercise both with myself and with clients. I try to incorporate a short version of the exercise into my weekly planning time. What am I avoiding this week that has an emotional punch? Can I unblock it? By integrating it into my regular routine, I become familiar with my recurring themes. This then helps me focus on small steps that can be built into my week to keep helping me move forward.

With clients, I have seen variations in terms of the types of responses people choose to put on their index cards. For some they are emotive: anger, frustration, sadness. For others, they are more behavioral: lack of motivation, passivity, impatience. What is most important is that the words on the cards represent the thought process of the client.

When that true connection is made, breakthroughs follow. I have also seen results by using this exercise at various levels: a quick run-through; a short but focused burst related to a certain project; or a more in-depth examination of some embedded issues that are complex and require time to unblock. Making our thoughts visible automatically means that we enter into a different relationship with them.

One of my clients had this to say about the exercise: "I was able to get to the core of my issues, and now I have a takeaway that will stay as sticky notes in my workspace for life! I thought that I knew what my sticking points were and how to fix them, but by getting everything down on cards, the themes were easily separated and answers presented themselves."

**

 About Midori Evans

Midori Evans is the founder of Midori Creativity, a coaching and consulting business in Westport, Massachusetts, that helps artists and businesspeople manifest their creative visions. She is fascinated by how we both create meaning and become our true selves. An experienced teacher and coach, she explores the world through writing, photography, and solo travel. . She has traveled to places as far-flung as Tunisia, Finland, and Japan and walked the Camino Frances through Spain. Midori Creativity offers private coaching, workshops, artist critique groups, and the Creativity Abloom conversation series. Visit midoricreativity.com, cedarlightimages.com, or email midori.creativity@gmail.com.

A Creative Ritual Exercise for Performance

48

Cynthia Holloway Kelvin

Exercise Purpose

This ritual is prescribed for those who need to perform in front of one or many people. It is also for actors at their "big" audition or for professionals who must stand in front of a crowd and perform by giving a talk or seminar. This creative ritual will help you clarify your gifts and support you in performing at your best when you need it the most.

 ## Exercise Description

Materials needed: blank piece of paper, pen, and a cool non-sugary beverage.

Ritual prescription: The first part of the ritual is putting pen to paper and allowing yourself to explore all of the expectations that you have around your performance or your ability to perform. Your exploration might go something like this:

+ I must be liked.
+ I need to appear smart.
+ I have to look like I'm in total control.
+ I should be funny.
+ I had better be entertaining.

 ## In Session or as Homework

Identify as many expectations as you can think of by writing them down in all directions on a blank piece of paper. Allow yourself to write without stopping, keeping up the pace so that you are writing whatever comes to mind. If you can't identify the expectations you or others have for your performance, then make them up! Yes, that's right, don't think, just make them up. You might be surprised by what you uncover.

Notice all the fears that surface in association with the expectations you have identified. These fears point to what you think you will experience as a result of not living up to the expectations you have identified. Notice what emotions are just under the fears, perhaps feelings of emotional anguish, humiliation, and the possible negative repercussions both personally and professionally that could result.

After you come up with all the expectations, fears, and emotions present, read them aloud, one by one, putting some real emotional expression into verbalizing each one. Now read them aloud again, this time dropping the feelings you have about each one and instead reading them in a neutral tone while repeating "that's interesting" after each one. Then take a slow sip from your cool beverage, savoring the liquid along with the thought, "that's interesting."

Continue to allow the judgments of these expectations, fears, and emotions you have identified to cool down. Work to neutralize these judgments as not being good or bad, just "interesting." Continue to recognize any judgmental thoughts, lightly considering them and letting go of your emotional attachment to them. Read, repeat, and sip until you feel neutral and complete.

Place your beverage to the side and put the paper in front of you. While looking at the words scrawled across the page in all directions, place your hands on your abdomen and take a nice, even breath through your nose and out through your mouth, sighing or letting out a sound on the exhale. Breathe in and out while making a sound on the exhale at least two more times.

Now spend a few moments just breathing nice, even breaths in through your nose and out through your nose. Imagine breathing in the coolness as you continue to take nice, even breaths, neither too shallow nor too fast or deep.

Once you are in a relaxed state, repeat the following:

+ "I release any expectations around my performance."
+ "I give myself permission to relax into my own unique expression."
+ "I release the need for perfection."
+ "I give myself all the confidence and courage I need to succeed."

If after you have repeated these statements in a relaxed state you are still unconvinced of what you are saying to yourself, place your hands on your chest, close your eyes or pick a point of soft focus on something in front of you, and repeat the phrase:

"I release the need for perfection."

As you remain with your eyes closed or with a soft focus, visualize driving to the venue. Watch your feet as you walk up the stairs to the stage, the lights overhead and the audience in front of you. Look out from the stage and see the faces of those to whom you are bringing your gift, some open and friendly, some tired but awake, some serious and skeptical, but all wanting you to succeed in sharing it with them.

Feel what it is like to be the center of attention, notice your body and breathe into any area that is holding tension. Just relax in the space between you and the audience, however big or small it may be, feeling all eyes on you. Breathe away any tension you still may be holding. If you are feeling really nervous, shake out your hands and let out a quick sigh with a sound. Then return to nice, even breaths.

Mentally review your environment. Feel yourself there: calm, cool, and collected. Stand with the knowledge that you are fully able to re-direct any feelings of nervousness into feelings of excitement. Now smile big at first and then an inward smile, feeling ready to share your gift with your audience. Look out at the audience, now seeing and feeling the gratitude they have at receiving this important gift. See the audience as open and grateful as you continue to breathe.

Take a step forward from where you are standing and begin the phrase: "I am . . ." Consider the gift that you most want to bring to your audience. Let a single word surface. Your phrase might become "I am . . . engaging," "I am . . . confident," or "I am . . . inspiring." Whatever this positive gift is, let it surface.

Repeat this phrase several times, really feeling the feelings that saying it evokes. Finish sipping your cool beverage, thinking about all the openness you feel from the audience. Feel the coolness of the glass in your hand, which is continuing to help you feel calm, cool, and collected as you play out the scene before you.

Now sit up or stand with your shoulders back while seeing, hearing, and feeling the applause as you stand there. Study the audience as they applaud. See their eyes, their smiling faces, and the nods of agreement to the person next to them. Take a bow. Yes, really, take a bow!

On the day of the performance, make yourself your cool beverage and repeat your "gift phrase" internally as you sip, gently repeating the phrase while relaxing with the cool glass in your hands. Allow yourself this time to get into your performance zone, and as you finish getting ready, continue to allow the phrase and the beverage to cool your nervous system.

After your performance, complete the ritual by making yourself your favorite warm beverage and spending a few moments reflecting on what you felt went well and what could have gone better. This will be especially helpful if you can write down everything in a journal. Allow yourself to explore all your thoughts on what occurred and how you felt about it.

Now write and read the following phrase aloud:

"I deserve credit for . . ."

Identify as many things as you can think of that you deserve to acknowledge about your performance, starting small and working your way towards what you really feel you did well. For example:

+ "I deserve credit for making it to the venue."
+ "I deserve credit for facing my fears and stepping on stage."
+ "I deserve credit for making it through the event."
+ "I deserve credit for smiling when I didn't feel like smiling at all."
+ "I deserve credit for giving my audience the gift of laughter."
+ "I deserve credit for sharing my wisdom in a way they could hear and understand."

Now continue to enjoy your warm beverage, reflecting on the warmth of those you engaged with before, during, and after, giving thanks for all the moments you are most happy with and for all the moments that helped you learn what to do differently next time. Then give yourself credit for doing this exercise and all the work you did behind the scenes to conquer your fears. You deserve the credit!

Remember you don't overcome performance anxiety by avoiding it. You get better as you work to actively find ways to move past fear and anxiety so as to share your gift of self-expression with others, on whatever size stage you choose to stand on.

 For Home Use

Because of the simple materials involved and the clear instructions, this is an excellent exercise to be employed for home use.

 Client Results

I've successfully used this powerful exercise with performers and with other clients, who uniformly find it valuable.

**

 About Cynthia Holloway Kelvin

Cynthia Holloway Kelvin is a licensed psychologist, registered drama therapist, and a performance consultant working with both performers and business professionals who are called on to perform for professional growth and personal evolution. She works with individuals in private practice performance consulting and offers group work through creative performance workshops. For more information about her work in performance consulting or creative performance workshops, find her online at The Evolving Stage (www. evolvingstage.com).

Mind-Movie Muse

49

Stephanie Bianchi

Exercise Purpose

Are you feeling blocked, uninspired, or just need to bust out of the cognitive/analytical box? If so, this exercise is for you.

 Exercise Description

Mind-Movie Muse is a simplified version of a method I use in my music therapy practice called the Bonny Method of Guided Imagery and Music. This exercise can help you access new levels of creativity and expanded awareness in a fun and unexpected way. Using music, it helps you tap into a deeper level of consciousness, somewhere between waking and dreaming, that frees your brain from its regular limiting thoughts, allowing you to experience new possibilities outside of your regular mental wheelhouse.

To prepare:

1. Plan a 20- to 30-minute chunk of uninterrupted time and space.
2. Download one (or all) of the pieces that are listed here onto your MP3 player into a separate playlist.
3. Cue the playlist so that all you have to do is hit "play."

Part 1. Induction

1. Settle into a comfortable position and close your eyes. For a few minutes, act as an observer of your thoughts, feelings, and bodily sensations. Just notice without judgment whatever is there.
2. Now draw your attention to your breathing, slowing down and elongating your exhales. Do eight full breaths, inhaling deeply on a slow four-count (1-2-3-4) and exhaling thoroughly on an eight-count (1-2-3-4-5-6-7-8). Count the breaths on your fingers if you need help keeping track.
3. After eight complete breaths, return to your normal breathing.

Part 2. Mind-Movie

1. See or sense in your mind's eye a movie screen in front of you. The lights dim, the curtain opens, and the screen lights up.
2. Press play on your music-playing device.
3. Letting the music guide your experience, watch what unfolds on the screen. Do not control or judge what comes up, simply watch.
4. After the music has ended, you may want to stay for the "credits."

Part 3. Movie Review

1. When you are ready to come back, slowly open your eyes and review the movie.
2. Either write a synopsis of your experience or draw pictures of the main scenes. Sometimes the best parts are in the details.
3. If you have thoughts or ideas about any part of your mind-movie, now is the time to review their implications.

Recommended Music:

For Exploration: Ottorino Respighi, "The Fountains of Rome" (I. Valle Giulia at Dawn, II. Triton Fountain at Morning, III. Trevi at Midday, IV. Villa Medici at Sunset)

For Emotional Processing: Johannes Brahms, "Concerto No. 2 in B-flat Major for Piano and Orchestra" (I. Allegro Non Troppo & III. Andante)

For Expansion: Ralph Vaughan Williams, "Fantasia on a Theme by Thomas Tallis," followed by "Symphony No. 5 in D Major" (III: Romanza, Lento)

For Activating Blocked Energy: Ludwig van Beethoven, "Symphony No. 7" (IV: Allegro Con Brio), followed by Alexander Borodin, "Prince Igor: Polovtsian Dances"

The pieces I have listed are just suggestions to get you started. If you have favorite pieces or songs that you know evoke imagery or inspire your imagination, try it with your own selections and make your own playlists. Let your subconscious muse guide you.

✸ In Session or as Homework

When I use guided imagery and music (GIM) in session with a client, the process is a bit different. The client verbalizes what she is experiencing, and I act as a chaperone of sorts, asking questions and offering support to help clarify and crystallize the experience.

If you try this with a client in session, act as an interested observer rather than as a therapist or guide. Asking questions like "What is happening now?" or "What is that like for you?" leaves the client space to let anything emerge without having to conjure images within specific parameters.

If you choose to give this exercise as homework, make sure to have your client write a "review" after the experience, so you can use this as a launching pad for analysis and conversation.

For Home Use

This exercise is perfectly suited either for in-session work or independent work at home.

Client Results

I do this exercise regularly for myself and with clients, and over the years it has elicited incredibly rewarding results. Basically, this is like dreaming while you're awake, or like intentional daydreaming, and allows you to let your analytical cognition go and just let your subconscious run wild for a bit.

It is also a safe way to work with deeper issues that may seem too difficult or delicate to handle in the regular conscious state. I have personally made deep realizations and discoveries about myself while doing this practice, and have witnessed some life-changing transformations in my clients that have translated into creative success.

For example, a songwriter I saw who was going through a divorce and had writer's block for months started doing this once a day, and suddenly the dam broke and the floodgates opened. She ended up writing a song a day for 30 days, and two of those songs ended up on *Billboard* charts.

**

About Stephanie Bianchi

Stephanie Bianchi is a board-certified music therapist, performance wellness coach, music director, voice-over actor, and composer/lyricist. She has written and performed music and lyrics for a variety of TV and radio shows and ads, independent films, children's videos, and educational programs. She believes music is the most powerful healing agent we have, and uses it as the main tool in helping to create positive, lasting change in her clients. She has a private music therapy practice in New York City and has helped many musicians, actors, dancers, and writers break through mental and emotional barriers that prohibit optional functioning and performance.

For more information, please visit her website: www.StephanieBianchi.com

For more information on the Bonny Method of GIM, please visit: www.ami-bonnymethod.org

For more information on music therapy, please visit: www.musictherapy.org

Creative Problem-Solving Using Tree and Nature Images

50

Jackee Holder

Exercise Purpose

Trees are associated with generative and often restorative associations including balance, alignment, rhythms and cycles, loss, and resilience. Trees remind us of the natural elements of growth. Yet the frantic pace of daily life means that it is easy to rely on what we have always done rather than making time and space to discover new and novel ways of responding to creative blocks and stresses.

   Creating space as part of your creative practice to step back and reflect is a positive tool for creatives to embody. Working creatively with tree and nature images as well as associated metaphors sparks significant and sometimes evocative memories that, when given time and space, galvanize right-brain thinking, allowing exploration of issues and themes from a more organic and intuitive perspective.

 Exercise Description

The reflective and intuitive approach of this exercise means it can be applied to almost any creative block, challenge, or dilemma.

   Step 1. Advance prep supports creating the right space for getting creative with this exercise. Decide on what the question or block is you want help with. Next, collect ten or more different and varied images of trees. You may want to print these out or have them open as images on your desktop or digital device.

   Step 2. The next step is to choose an image to work with. You will need a notebook and pen or something to write with for the next steps. Choose a tree image that appeals to you and free-write, draw, or whatever feels right in response to the questions below as a way of inquiry into the presenting issue you are working with.

1. What are your first immediate thoughts and responses to your tree image?
2. What memories does the image conjure up?
3. How are you feeling in your body as you observe and connect with the image?

Step 3. Next, consider any parallels, connections, similarities, or differences that the tree image stimulates in relation to your creative block or work or life issue or dilemma.

Step 4. Now deepen into your inquiry by using the prompts that follow to explore the image as it relates to your issue in more detail. Feel free to go with your own questions and prompts.

1. How is the tree in your image a metaphor or reflection of how you currently feel about your issue?
2. How is it reflecting how or where you want to be with your issue?
3. What specific aspect of where you want to be is reflected in your tree's energy or physical appearance?
4. What do you imagine the roots of the tree see from deep underground in relation to your issue that might not be visible to you right now?
5. What data might the tree's leaves that have not yet blossomed know about potential possibilities or solutions that are about to become open to you?
6. Imagine your tree sharing its worldly wisdom with you. What ideas does it have about how you might go about responding to your issue differently?

Step 5. Visualization can deepen the impact of this creative practice by activating the imagination to expand and explore different perspectives. Using the archetype of the inner wise self is another approach to working with this creative practice. Imagine that your inner wise self was sitting next to you on a branch of this tree. The two of you are in conversation. Play out the conversation and guidance this inner wise part of yourself is saying to you. What would this part of your inner wise self be encouraging and motivating you to do or be at this time?

Be observant for even the smallest sign or detail. Capture what you hear, sense, or feel in writing, by drawing, or in bullet points. Encourage yourself to not censor or judge what you hear or connect with at this stage. Treat everything as potential possibilities (however unformed the clues and signals might seem) that can be turned into informed action.

As you come to the end of the practice, explore the following question to gather any meaningful connections or observations that have come from the practice: How could you connect more with your tree wisdom and inner wise self creatively in the future?

Think of both your "tree wisdom" and "inner wise self" as creative, resourceful parts of the self that you can freely access whenever you feel frustrated, stuck, or overwhelmed creatively.

Step 6. Remind yourself as you engage with this practice that creative solutions often don't arrive in linear, logical formats. Boost this exercise by free-writing and expressing yourself in other creative ways that feel natural or organic. Give yourself sufficient time to capture your responses in an unhurried fashion. It can be helpful to set an alarm, for example, for 15 minutes, and remain open to continuing after the alarm goes off if you find yourself in a flow.

Step 7. The reflection time after this practice is crucial. Leave time to reflect afterwards on the experience and what emerged during the practice. You might find yourself surprised by what the right brain connects with that is outside of your logical and rational mind. This part of the process is about sifting through the data to find what is illuminated. Failure to commit to this stage of the practice often means that you lose valuable solutions that are not at first glance overtly obvious.

 In Session or as Homework

This exercise can be facilitated and introduced into one-on-one sessions, as individual development work, or as part of supervision, team development, and group sessions. It can be used with creatives or to foster creativity with individuals and teams. As a self-managed creative approach, it empowers individuals with the choice to take charge of the reins of connecting with their own personal power and inner resourcefulness.

You can adapt the exercise in a variety of ways. For example, a tree image could be chosen randomly or intentionally when working with groups and teams. For example, when working with groups and teams, I display a selection of tree images around the room and invite individuals to intentionally select an image to work with. Or they are given a choice to select a tree image that is not visible and is tucked away in a sealed envelope.

When working virtually, you can share the images on screen or email in advance and invite individuals to choose a tree image from the selection. When working with large groups at conferences, we place a random tree image in an envelope and place it under each delegate chair. This simple action creates an air of intrigue and wonder.

Ritual and ceremony subliminally become part of the process of working with tree and nature images, and it is wonderful to hear the memories and stories that are unearthed and given voice to as people work with the images in ways that feel natural and true.

A short free-writing exercise around an early tree or nature memory can help individuals warm up. Let participants know not to worry about grammar or punctuation, so that this does not add to the feeling of being creatively blocked. The prompts are a guide but not mandatory. Start where the people you work with are. Give yourself permission to go with what unfolds.

If you plan to use this approach as a practitioner, make sure you try it out yourself to get a feel for how it works. Even more important is to observe your own resistances and any anxiety you experience so you can be aware of any parallel processes that might also be present in individuals and groups you are working with. Stepping away from logical thinking can increase anxiety for many individuals, so stay open and flexible and use your skill and expertise when working one-on-one or with teams and introduce the exercise with a light, sensitive, and empathetic touch.

 For Home Use

As mentioned earlier, this exercise is perfect for individual development work at home.

Client Results

As I indicated, this exercise can be facilitated and introduced into one-on-one sessions, as individual development work, or as part of supervision, team development, and group sessions. Clients and participants in each of these categories have found this exercise to be effective and valuable.

**

 ## About Jackee Holder

London born and raised, Jackee loves the diversity and richness of urban living. Her multi-layered portfolio includes her work as a writer and published author, creativity coaching, and facilitation of leadership and well-being courses and workshops. She speaks at conferences and events, adding her voice to what feeds and nourishes our souls and spirits. A nature and tree lover, she brings the world of nature into her work at every opportunity and sees that as the voice of her creative spirit at work. She is the curator and host of the online "Paper Therapy" course and is currently hard at work on her fifth book.

Website: www.jackeeholder.com
Email: info@jackeeholder.com
Twitter: @jackeeholder

Symbols of the Season

51

Nora Sibley

Exercise Purpose

This exercise helps creatives connect with their senses and the season as a vehicle for building personal meaning in the work. By connecting the physical and mental associations, new creative sparks fly and inspired, meaningful action can take place.

 Exercise Description

Creatives are prompted to bring their awareness to the changing seasons by first sitting down to journal their responses to some questions. Next, they are asked to gather physical materials that relate to the thoughts and feelings that came up in the journaling exercise. The mental associations that arise bring additional meaning to the still-life objects they gather. When studied together, the answers to their questions and the objects they've gathered are potentially worthy of further reflection and creative action.

Step 1. Journaling. Here are the questions that creatives are asked to journal on for about 15 minutes:

+ How do you acknowledge the changing seasons?
+ Are there any feelings that the current season brings up for you?
+ Do you perform any rituals this time of year that build meaning for you?
+ Is there any sense of nostalgia for you that this season engenders?
+ What scents and sounds of the season excite you or bring you comfort?
+ Is there a favorite food you like to enjoy during this season?
+ Is there a favorite activity you like to enjoy during this season?
+ Is there any activity or place that you want to revisit?

Creatives are then given the following instruction: look back over the words in your journal and underline any phrases or words that jump out at you. Do you feel the energy of any colors in your mind as you read over your notes? Reflect on any emotions that you might have been holding back on. Would you consider going any deeper?

Step 2. Going into the season. Creatives are given the following instructions:

Go outside, take a short walk into a natural landscape, and sit somewhere comfortable. Close your eyes. Breathe in slowly.

+ Is the air warm or cool?
+ Do you smell anything in particular?
+ What do you hear?

The goal is to be fully present in this moment in time. Let all your senses guide you in acknowledging what is unique to this time of year.

Step 3. Collection and illustration. Collect a couple of items or materials that reflect the current season. They can be from nature or from around your home, or even from the grocery store. Choose whatever you are drawn to.

Set up a simple still life of the objects. Illustrate them in whatever medium you prefer without worrying about your skills as an artist.

Think about why you chose them. Was it the color, shape, taste, texture? Was it about the memories attached to them or the meaning they hold for you?

As you *really see* them, what are you thinking about? Can you "illustrate" and infuse your work with these thoughts and feelings?

In Session or as Homework

I use this exercise as an art prompt that creatives can attempt on their own. Clients who are struggling with anxiety or who are feeling a loss of meaning in their art practice find this exercise to be a simple way to get the creative juices flowing again. We then devote the next session to exploring what came up and whether it was useful in getting them started with art-making again.

For Home Use

Getting out of the studio space and taking a walk outside relaxes a creative's mind and body and can help an artist reconnect with themselves and their senses. Being in a quiet, natural environment and breathing fresh air helps thoughts and feelings from the journaling practice sink in.

When we were children, nature filled us with curiosity and inspiration. As adults, we want to reignite these feelings of wonder that are quite easy to access, wherever we find ourselves. The crossroads of thought, association, memory, exploration, and personality, I find, encourage action and meaning making.

Once the objects are chosen and the art-making has begun, try changing perspective, lighting, materials, the size of the drawing, etc.

Client Results

With several older clients who were struggling with whether their art practice was still meaningful to them, this exercise helped them find a way back to just *seeing* and creating in a simple way. Further, they noted that the exercise of thinking about what held meaning for them in a larger sense, including their traditions and rituals, created a natural bridge to meaningful subjects worthy of their attention and creativity.

One client of mine was very excited to have been given this prompt. The self-portrait work she regularly pursued created a lot of anxiety, and her blocks worsened as she aged. The invitation to explore *any* other subject matter would probably have been received well, but this particular prompt to gather objects and think about the current season was particularly grounding, enjoyable, and lighter emotionally.

She welcomed the opportunity and easily started producing work as a result. She enjoyed playing with the lighting and the shadows and really looking and seeing her objects. These objects included colorful fruits that were connected for her to childhood memories of the holiday season. I believe that she felt a renewed sense of wonder and awe and appreciation for her art practice.

Tackling this new subject matter also meant that she bought a new tube of paint in a bright orange color. This step—adding new materials to her toolkit—also felt like a successful result, as it meant that she was open to new paths and potential projects. As we wrapped up our sessions, she shared that she was "thrilled" with her new series of works in pen, charcoal, and paint.

I have found that the more my clients are connected with their senses, the natural world, and their memories and experiences, the less anxiety is part of the process of art-making for them and the more meaningful the end result.

**

 About Nora Sibley

Nora Sibley is a Rhode Island School of Design graduate, an artist, interior decorator, and a lover of vibrant color and inspiring travel. Currently she is a San Francisco–based creative director and creativity coach, supporting artists in cultivating their intuition, sense awareness, and inner resources. Visit her at www.norasibley.com or nora@norasibley.com.

Creative Alchemy **52**

Pragati Chaudhry

Exercise Purpose

This exercise uses colors to alchemize gremlins by awakening a creative's sensory, non-verbal intelligence. Breakthroughs in brain science are now confirming that the nonverbal portion of the brain plays a significant role in processing information. Creative Alchemy exercises facilitate a re-connection with the inner healer inside of us and help creatives overcome unwanted beliefs and blocks.

 ## Exercise Description

A simple creative act, as simple as splashing color on paper, has given survivors of trauma a voice of release. In those situations, verbal coaching and therapy could not assist them because trauma survivors couldn't use their words. Engaging the nonverbal portion of the brain allowed them to communicate and restore homeostasis.

 ## In Session and as Homework

Step 1. Preparation

1. Plan for a 35- to 40-minute period of uninterrupted time.
2. Bring some liquid acrylic colors, Q-tips, and cardstock paper.
3. Bring a timer.

Step 2. Warm Up

1. Seat yourself comfortably at a table and for a few minutes close your eyes and notice what comes up. Images will come up and words will come up; without judgment,

write down the first three words. They don't need to connect or to make sense together as these are warm-up words.

2. After you have written those three words, draw your attention to your first word and choose three colors. You don't want to expand the palette of colors beyond three, because that will limit spontaneity and will bring attention to visual appeal. Clients use Q-tips for the same reason, because artist brushes or palette knives can limit the spontaneity of raw expression.

3. Then think of the second word you wrote and see or sense in your mind's eye what colors it brings up. A visual splash of colors usually comes up, which equates to feelings brought up by the word in your brain. Without effort, your brain begins to work with accepting and acknowledging those feelings as you engage in the exercise. For instance, if the word is "stressed," I notice that engaging with its colors immediately starts the release of that stress. It's an allowance and acknowledgement of the stressful issue that allows its charge to dissipate.

4. For no longer than 2 minutes per word, express yourself with color and Q-tips on paper. After every word, take a fresh piece of paper and move on to the next word in your list. When you are done with the third warm-up word, please put your papers and Q-tips to the side.

Step 3. Diving Into the Issue

When you are ready, close your eyes and take a few breaths to connect with the issue that brought you to coaching. We will work with this issue now, in five sections, all of them on one sheet of paper.

Once you've connected with your issue, open your eyes, pick three colors, and respond to the following five prompts, spending no more than 5 minutes on each prompt and doing all of your work on a single sheet of paper:

1. What is this?
2. How is this affecting my life?
3. Is there a gift in this?
4. Imagine yourself on a conveyer belt, moving through and past this, and coming out to the other side. What do you see?
5. Where do I go from here?

Through this Creative Alchemy exercise, we can make contact with the infinite source of support and well-being that is available from within. We can discover our blocks without resistance or denial, experience extraordinary clarity, and release unwanted beliefs. This happened to Sonia, a client of mine (discussed shortly).

 For Home Use

This exercise is ideally suited for home use.

Client Results

Sonia enjoyed painting and loved to express her creativity, but a tragedy changed the course of her life and her ability to express herself. It affected her in so many ways, but losing contact with her creative impulse and abilities was a major blow. She went to therapy and self-help groups but found herself getting too comfortable with her familiar use of words: once she got comfortable in therapy, Sonia used her words to appease rather than release.

With Creative Alchemy, Sonia found herself unable to use her familiar words. She had to deal with her issue nonverbally and she experienced the energy of her issue as she dipped the Q-tips into paint and colored whatever came up. She took the opportunity to sink into all the unpleasantness and register the feelings that she had resisted before.

After finishing the exercise, Sonia revealed that she was a victim of cyber fraud and identity theft. Despite her legal efforts, she could not erase the effects of the fraud on her professional life. She felt like a victim whose voice wasn't heard and, as one result, she stopped expressing herself through art.

Even though she had tried to come out the other side of this experience through therapy and self-help groups, Sonia hadn't been able to. With the Creative Alchemy exercise, though, she was able to allow her nonverbal brain to bring her much-needed healing.

Sonia came to the second session with the report that she started painting! She was calm and really happy to return to art and to allow herself to be at ease again. During the second session, she saw herself getting off the conveyor belt and, as a result of that visualization, she allowed her "victim" identity to fully pass on. Engaging the nonverbal portion of brain allowed Sonia to reclaim her power.

**

About Pragati Chaudhry

Pragati Chaudhry holds a degree in Fine Arts (MFA) and in Teaching Fine Arts (MST), and loves leading people to a space where they stop creating from struggle and start reclaiming their true power. She has had the privilege of working with extraordinary people from all around the world who have followed their calling to connect with their own creative alchemy. Trained as a creativity coach and having studied trauma-informed expressive arts therapy, she offers coaching and workshops for deep transformation through art and writing. She facilitates Creative Alchemy "Healing With Art" workshops online and in Atlanta, Georgia: www.creativealchemies.com.

Freedom Within Form

53

Ann Boyd

Exercise Purpose

This exercise explores the intentional use of constraints to inspire freedom of expression. Freedom Within Form invites creatives to craft "constraints" or "rules" to free their intuitive voices. This exercise can become a practice that strengthens creativity, generates new and surprising ideas, and helps creatives to develop a playful relationship to the inevitable constraints of time, resources, space, etc.

 Exercise Description

Preparation

Materials: You will need a timer, an unlined notebook or sketchbook, and a favorite writing instrument that allows you to write quickly and easily.

Environment: Explore working in various environments with varying amounts of time. If you consider yourself someone who needs quiet to focus, stretch yourself to write in a busy café and vice versa.

Centering: Before you begin, take a moment (or more) to bring yourself into the present moment. You may have your own way of centering, but here are a few offerings.

1. Three Breaths: Give yourself the gift of three breaths. Close your eyes. As you inhale invite the word or image of Opening, and as you exhale invite the word or image of Softening.
2. Observing Through the Senses: Take a moment to observe your surroundings, take note of the light, the colors, the sounds, the smells, the textures, the temperature, etc. You can do this inwardly or set your timer for one minute and jot down one-word observations of what you are experiencing through your senses.
3. Rooting: Place your feet squarely on the ground as you sit. With your inner eye, imagine the energy gently moving into the ground like the roots of a tree. See the energy rooting through the chair, through the floor, into the earth. As you root your energy down, see a golden light moving up your spine and out through the crown of your head beaming into the dark space. Breathe there for a moment.

Step 1. Create Your Constraints

Constraints or "rules" are always a factor in our creative practices, whether we are consciously aware of them or not. The sonnet, destina, limerick, and haiku are all examples of traditional constraint-based writing practices. In this exercise, we actively create constraints in order to bypass our inner critics and habits of expression to arrive at fresh and surprising material.

Set your timer for one minute. We give ourselves a time limit in order to dive in without overthinking our choices.

Begin by writing the date at the top of your page. Using the numbers in the date as our guide, we can create constraints. For example, today as I write this, it is 10/25/2019. I might constrain my writing to contain:

+ 10 lines
+ 2 wishes
+ 5 rhymes
+ 2 sounds
+ 0 people
+ 1 fox
+ 9 words in alliteration

Step 2. Write

Set the timer for the number of minutes you would like to offer yourself. In this case I am only looking to write ten lines, so perhaps 5 minutes is enough. In any case, work to finish your writing "recipe" within your given time frame.

Though you can use a computer for this work, explore working with paper and pen. There are many studies that investigate the differences between writing by hand and on a keyboard. I invite you to incorporate the hand-to-heart-to-mind connection of physically writing.

Begin by free-writing. Paraphrasing Natalie Goldberg's free-writing rules, write quickly, without stopping, without erasing, without crossing out, without any worries about spelling or grammar, without second-guessing yourself, and without censoring yourself.

You may be able to free-write and simultaneously fulfill the constraints you've set for yourself, or you may use the text created in your free-write to fulfill your constraints. Either way, satisfy all of your constraints and nothing more within the time frame.

Step 3. Loop

You might create a second piece of writing inspired by your first piece. Choose a word, phrase, or line that inspires you. Create new constraints. The date is a fun and useful structure for generating constraints, but creating constraints can be as much of its own creative practice as the writing itself.

In Session or as Homework

Freedom Within Form can be used as a warm-up for any sort of class or workshop and helps participants focus energy and generate text. If you are a coach, I would recommend that you work with the exercise yourself, exploring various environments, constraints, and time frames. Once you have developed a personal relationship to the exercise, you will feel more confident in leading a client through it during a session and inviting them to work with the exercise as a daily practice.

Freedom Within Form is fluid in that the constraint choices are endless and can be shaped to work specifically with content that challenges or interests the individual. Initially the constraints can feel like a burden or can even inspire a kind of fear of failure, but ultimately clients find this work to be inspiring and freeing.

As you and/or your clients get comfortable crafting constraints and embracing the structure that this exercise offers, you can adapt these ideas to any medium. Constraints become a conscious part of your practice and a great source of inspiration.

For Home Use

Given the exercise's easy requirements—just a timer, an unlined notebook or sketchbook, and a favorite writing instrument that allows you to write quickly and easily—it's well-suited for home use.

 Client Results

I have worked with variations of this exercise in class settings and with my own practice for so long now that it is an integral part of both my teaching and creative practices. I have watched students who are paralyzed by an empty page totally embrace working with constraints and find a freedom in their writing. This creative freedom translates to other mediums and invites practitioners into a less critical, more open-hearted space that recognizes even the most mundane moments as rich with detail and opportunity for creative exploration.

**

 About Ann Boyd

Ann Boyd is a long-time creative who made theatre and taught for many years at Columbia College Chicago. She now lives in Bend, Oregon, with her family, where she writes, enjoys working with people one-on-one on their creative practice, farms, and teaches theatre at the Waldorf School of Bend. If you are interested in working with Ann, you can contact her directly at boydland22@sbcglobal.net.

Index